EVERYDAY CIRCLE TIMES

by
Liz & Dick Wilmes
art
Jeane Healy

A **BUILDING BLOCKS** Publication

BOX 31 · DUNDEE · ILLINOIS · 60118

ISBN 0-943452-01-5
Library of Congress Catalog No. 83-071169

BOOK LIST COMPILED BY:
JILL BRADISH, Librarian
GAIL BORDEN LIBRARY
Elgin, Illinois 60120

PUBLISHED BY:
BUILDING BLOCKS
P.O. Box 31
Dundee, Illinois 60118

DISTRIBUTED BY:
GRYPHON HOUSE, Inc.
P.O. Box 275
Mt. Rainier, MD 20712

ISBN 0-943452-01-5

DEDICATED TO

... all young children who learn and grow everyday and to their teachers who stimulate and encourage this growth

Contents

SCHOOL BEGINS

FOR OPENERS

BEFORE SCHOOL BEGINS GET A LARGE BRANCH. MIX A BIG BUCKET OF PLASTER OF PARIS. PUT THE BRANCH IN THE PLASTER. LET IT HARDEN.

HAVE THIS SPECIAL TREE IN THE CIRCLE TIME AREA. TAKE EACH CHILD'S PICTURE THAT FIRST DAY. TELL THE CHILDREN THAT WHEN THE PICTURES ARE DEVELOPED YOU ARE GOING TO HANG THEM ON THE TREE FOR EVERYONE TO ENJOY. WHEN DEVELOPED, PUNCH A HOLE NEAR THE TOP OF EACH ONE AND LOOP A PIECE OF BRIGHTLY COLORED YARN FOR HANGING.

EXTENSION: CHANGE THIS TREE THROUGHOUT THE YEAR TO HIGHLIGHT VARIOUS SEASONS, THEMES, AND HOLIDAYS.

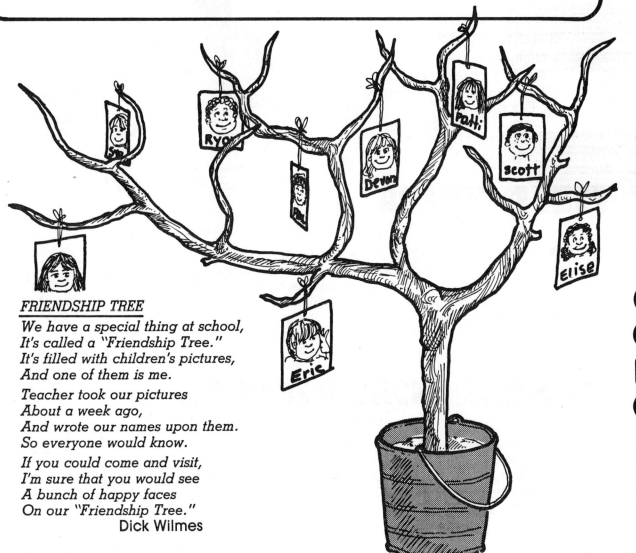

FRIENDSHIP TREE

We have a special thing at school,
It's called a "Friendship Tree."
It's filled with children's pictures,
And one of them is me.

Teacher took our pictures
About a week ago,
And wrote our names upon them.
So everyone would know.

If you could come and visit,
I'm sure that you would see
A bunch of happy faces
On our "Friendship Tree."
　　　　　　　Dick Wilmes

SELF CONCEPT

FINGERPLAYS

SCHOOL FRIENDS

Today was the day
For school to begin.
We met our new teacher,
Who talks with a grin.

There is Amy and Sue,
Keith, Kevin and Paul.
As hard as I try
I still can't remember them all.

It's really exciting
To have some new friends.
I'll know all their names
Before the school ends.
        Dick Wilmes

NEW FRIENDS

So many children
It's going to be fun.
They know their own name,
But I only know one.
        Dick Wilmes

RECIPES

SIMPLE BEGINNERS

Stuffed Celery
Apple Slices with Peanut Butter
Mixed Raisins, Nuts, Seeds,
   Coconut, etc.
Crackers and Cheese
Hard Boiled Egg Half

FIELD TRIPS

● During the first week of school take several walks around the facility. The children need to feel comfortable with their surroundings so they will enjoy coming to school each day. During the Inside Walk show the children where the washrooms, drinking fountains, office, outside doors, and other necessary equipment and rooms are. During the Outside Walk, concentrate on the playground, playground equipment, and any safety signs that the children need to obey each day.

CLASSROOM VISITOR

● Many people other than the teacher and aides help the children each day. During the first several weeks have these people introduce themselves to the children and tell them what they do while the children are in the classroom. These visits do not have to be long, but they will help the children understand how many people are at the school helping to make each day a good one.

LANGUAGE GAMES

TALK ABOUT   During the first week of school, take the children around the room and introduce them to the equipment, materials, and storage facilities in the room. Talk about how to use the learning centers, how to handle the materials and supplies and how to be safe. Include any specific directions for the particular learning centers.

SECRET PICTURES   Before circle time, cut out large pictures from catalogs of different pieces of equipment and major supplies which the children will use — puzzles, blocks, balls, paint, clay, brushes, dolls, the climber, books, felt board, magnets, easel, scissors, and so on. Glue each picture onto a piece of construction paper. Then put a piece of paper over each picture so that the children cannot see what it is. Tape the paper to the construction paper along the left side. Cut the top piece of paper into 5 or 6 strips so that it remains taped along the left edge.

Bring the 'secret pictures' to circle time. Say to the children, *"I have brought pictures of the things that you have seen and played with in our classroom. You are really going to need your brain to figure out what each one is.* (Hold the first one up.) Ask, *"Can anyone tell what this is a picture of?"* Of course the answer will be *"No!"* since the children can't see any part of the picture. *"Watch carefully, I'm going to uncover a little more of the picture.* (Fold over one strip so that the children can see a part of the picture.) *Can anybody tell what it is now?* (Let them guess.) *I'm going to uncover a little more of the picture. Can you guess now?"* Let them guess again. Continue until they have guessed what the picture is. Then talk about how to use that piece of equipment or supply. Enjoy this activity over several days as a review of how to use the things in the classroom.

SELF CONCEPT

ACTIVE GAMES

BASIC SKILLS

Children need to learn many skills to play the active games throughout the year:

- PASSING OBJECTS: One of the most basic skills is to pass an object to the person next to them. Start passing beanbags around the circle. Go slowly at first. As the children are passing, you can clap to give them a sense of rhythm. As the children understand how to pass the beanbag around the circle, change the rhythm of the passing by clapping at different speeds or playing music.

- MOVING AROUND THE CIRCLE: Start the children moving in a circle by doing simple movements without music. For example, have the children hold hands and walk around the circle. After several times around, have them slide around. Do these and other basic movements at different speeds. After a week or so, add music.

- PARACHUTE PLAY: You can buy a lightweight parachute or use a double bed sheet. This is one of the most exciting and versatile activities that you can play with young children. It is very important however that you work slowly with them at first until they know the basic holds, positions, and several simple moves. Once they know these, they can enjoy the variety of parachute games suggested throughout this book.

ACTIVE GAMES

ARACHUTE PLAY

- HOLDS
  - Have the children hold the parachute with both hands *'fists up'*.
  - Have them hold the parachute with both hands *'fist down'*.
  - Hold the parachute with one hand *'fist up'* and the other *'fist down'*.
  - Have them hold the parachute with *'arms crossed.'*
- POSITIONS
  - Have the children sitting.
  - Have the children kneeling.
  - Have the children standing.
- SIMPLE MOVES
  - Holding the parachute with both hands *('fists up'* and then *'fists down'*), have the children walk around in a circle. Watch to be certain that all of the children are holding the parachute exactly as you directed. Once they can do this, have them use one hand while walking. Now that they can control the parachute, practice going in one direction, stopping, and then reversing their stride by going in the opposite direction.
  - Staying in one place, have the children *'wave'* the parachute. *'Wave'* slowly at first. When this motion is under control vary the speed.
  - Practice stopping throughout the moves. It is very important that the children listen to all of the directions.

BOOKS

ELIZABETH BRAM — *I DON'T WANT TO GO TO SCHOOL*
HARLOW ROCKWELL — *MY NURSERY SCHOOL*

SELF CONCEPT

MY BODY

FOR OPENERS

AT ART LET EACH CHILD MAKE A PAIR OF BINOCULARS BY GLUING TWO TOILET PAPER ROLLS TOGETHER AND LOOPING A PIECE OF YARN SO IT CAN HANG AROUND THE CHILD'S NECK. DECORATE.

HAVE THE CHILDREN BRING THEIR BINOCULARS TO CIRCLE TIME. THE CHILDREN SHOULD SIT FACING EACH OTHER IN PAIRS. HAVE ONE CHILD IN EACH PAIR LOOK THROUGH HIS / HER BINOCULARS AT HIS / HER PARTNER. WHILE LOOKING THROUGH THE BINOCULARS S/HE SAYS "I'M LOOKING AT YOUR ARM." THE SECOND CHILD THEN POINTS TO HIS / HER ARM. THEY SWITCH AND THE SECOND CHILD LOOKS THROUGH HIS / HER BINOCULARS AND NAMES A BODY PART AND THE FIRST CHILD POINTS TO IT. SWITCH BACK AND FORTH SEVERAL TIMES.

FINGERPLAYS

ALL BY MYSELF
There are many things that I can do,
All by myself.
I can comb my hair and lace my shoe,
All by myself.
I can wash my hands and clean my face,
All by myself.
I can put my toys and blocks in place,
All by myself.

TEN LITTLE FINGERS
I have ten little fingers,
They all belong to me.
I can make them do things,
Would you like to see?

I can close them up tight.
I can open them up wide.
I can hold them up high.
I can put them at my side.
I can wave them to and fro.
And I can hold them just so.

TWO LITTLE HANDS
Two little hands go clap, clap, clap.
Two little feet go tap, tap, tap.
Two little hands go thump, thump, thump.
Two little feet go jump, jump, jump.
One little body turns round and round.
And sits quietly down.

REACH FOR THE CEILING
Reach for the ceiling,
Touch the floor,
Stand up again,
Let's do some more.

Touch your head,
Touch your knee,
Up to your shoulders,
Like this, you see?

Reach for the ceiling,
Touch the floor,
That's all for now,
There is no more.

RECIPES

PEOPLE
YOU'LL NEED

Ingredients for your favorite ginger bread or graham cracker recipe.
'People' cookie cutters

TO MAKE: Make the dough with your children according to the directions. Roll out the dough and let each child make a 'person'. Talk about the legs, head, arms, etc. on the cookie. If you want let the children decorate their cookies with nuts and raisins before baking.

THUMB PRINT COOKIES
YOU'LL NEED

2 cups of flour
1 t. salt
⅔ cup of oil
4-5 T. water

TO MAKE: Put all of the ingredients into a bowl. Mix with your hands or a fork. Roll the dough into small balls. Press your thumb into the center of each ball. Bake on a greased cookie sheet at 325 degrees for 10 minutes. Let cool and then fill with jam or peanut butter.

FIELD TRIPS

● Each time you walk out to the playground have the children gather in a special way to accent body differences and similiarities:

    Shortest to tallest (reverse)
    Blondes first, then those with brown hair, black hair, red hair, etc.
    (vary the order each time)
    Color of their eyes

CLASSROOM VISITOR

● Call the organization in your town which does vision and hearing screenings for young children. Have a volunteer come out to the center and screen all of the children.

SELF CONCEPT

13

LANGUAGE GAMES

BODY PARTS
: Have large pictures of body parts. Hold up each picture. Have the children call out the name of the part.

GUESS THE BODY PART
: • Get a large sheet of paper. Have a child come to the front of the circle and the others close their eyes. Cover up one of the child's 'legs'. Have the others open their eyes and quietly call out what part is covered up. Do this several more times with other large body parts.
: • Have another child come up. Get a small piece of paper. Cover up an 'ear'. Let the children guess what part is covered up. Continue with other smaller body parts.
: • Have a child come up to the front of the circle. Have him/her point to a body part and say, "I'm pointing to my _____." The group fills in the blank and then they point to that part on themselves. Continue in this manner using different children as leaders.

CLOSE EXAMINATION
: Have pairs of children sit facing each other. Have one child in each pair make 'binoculars' with his/her hands. While looking through the 'binoculars', have him/her describe the other child. While the children are doing this, walk around the group and encourage them to talk about facial features and other body parts. Switch. Let the partner make 'pretend binoculars' and describe the first child.

RIDDLES
: Say riddles to the children such as, "I'm thinking of the body part that you put your socks and shoes over. What is it?" or "It's on your face. You use it to eat and talk with. What is it?"

14

LANGUAGE GAMES

FOLLOW DIRECTIONS   Ask one child to come up and face the group. Whisper directions to him/her, such as *"Wiggle your leg."* As the child is following the directions, have the group name the part of the body the child is moving. Taking turns, continue to play the game using all of the body parts that your children are learning.
VARIATION:
Have a child come to the front of the circle. Have him/her stand still. Then whisper a body part to him/her. All of the children should watch carefully. S/he briefly moves that part and then stands quietly again. The children call out which body part s/he moved. Let the child do this several times and then give others the opportunity.

LISTEN CAREFULLY   During the first part of the week have a tape recorder and mirror out during free play. Have each child describe him/herself into the recorder. S/he can talk about his/her face, clothes, favorite toys, etc. If the child is having difficulty, encourage conversation by asking questions like:
"What color hair do you have?"
"Tell me about the clothes that you're wearing."
After you have taped each child's voice, play the tape at circle time. Have the class guess who is talking.

ACTIVE GAMES

RELAXING   Try some relaxation routines, such as hanging like a rag doll, simple yoga-type or isometric exercises.

SELF CONCEPT

ACTIVE GAMES

MOVING

Move around the circle doing different activities:
- Hold arms stiff while walking.
- Swing arms back and forth.
- Wiggle noses.
- Shake hands.
- March.

THINK AND
MOVE

Have the children try to think of different ways to move their body parts. For example begin by discussing *'legs'*. *"How many ways can you think of to move your legs?* (Walking, hopping, swinging, bending) *Can you think of any other ways to move your legs?* (If your group of children is beginning to understand the written word, make a list as you do this game.) *Now that we have thought of all of these ways to move our legs, let's try movng them in all of these ways."* Repeat this game on other days using different body parts such as *'arm'*, *'head'*, *'fingers'*, *'mouth'*, and so on.

OBSTACLE
COURSE

Set up an *'inside'* obstacle course with equipment from the classroom. Talk with the children about the body parts that they are using as they go through the course. *"You'll need to pull with your arms as you scoot under the table."* or *"You're crawling on your knees."*

ACTIVE GAMES

NO
TOUCHING

In a large open area, have the children walk around without touching each other. Have a signal when to start and stop.
VARIATION:
Give more specific directions, *"Move towards the closest wall without bumping into another person."* When the children know the game and can do it walking, use hopping, jumping, galloping, and sliding. These movements are more difficult to control.

SINGING

Sing

HEAD, SHOULDERS, KNEES, AND TOES
Head, shoulders, knees, and toes,
Knees and toes.
Head, shoulders, knees, and toes,
Knees and toes.
Eyes and ears and mouth and nose.

Sing

BEND AND STRETCH
Bend and stretch, reach for the stars.
There goes Jupiter.
Here comes Mars.
Bend and stretch, reach for the stars.
Stand on tip-e-toes,
Oh, so high!

BOOKS

BARBARA BRENNER — *BODIES*
JEAN HOLZENTHALER — *MY FEET DO*
JEAN HOLZENTHALER — *MY HANDS CAN*

SELF CONCEPT

CLOTHING

FOR OPENERS

HAVE A FULL LENGTH MIRROR AT CIRCLE TIME. HAVE ONE CHILD STAND IN FRONT OF IT. THE OTHER CHILDREN TAKE TURNS DESCRIBING A PIECE OF CLOTHING S/HE IS WEARING, SUCH AS "NICKY, YOU ARE WEARING SOMETHING RED AND WHITE." NICKY SHOULD LOOK AT HIMSELF IN THE MIRROR AND POINT TO THE PIECE OF CLOTHING AND SAY, "I AM WEARING RED AND WHITE SOCKS." AS YOU CONTINUE THE GAME, HAVE OTHER CHILDREN STAND IN FRONT OF THE MIRROR.

FINGERPLAYS

HELPING'S FUN

When I come in from outdoor play
I take my shoes off right away.
I set them by the door just so,
Then off my scarf and hat they go.
Zip down my coat and sweater too
And hang them up when I am through.
I'll leave them there 'till I go out
After lunch without a doubt.

TYING MY SHOE

I know how to tie my shoe.
I take the loop and poke it through.
It's very hard to make it stay,
Because my thumb gets in the way.

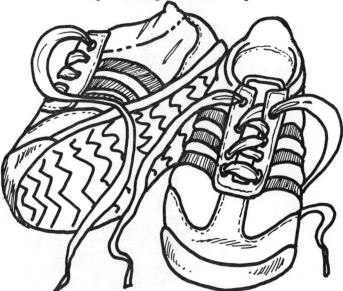

RECIPES

PEOPLE

YOU'LL NEED

Your favorite sugar cookie ingredients
2 egg whites
Several drops of water
Different food colorings

TO MAKE: Make your favorite sugar cookie recipe. Roll the dough out. Using people cookie cutters, let each child make a person. Bake according to your directions. When the cookies have baked, make "paint" for the children to frost the cookies.

Blend the egg whites and water. Divide the mixture among several bowls. Add a different food coloring into each bowl. Let the children "paint" clothes on their cookie.

CLASSROOM VISITOR

● Ask a parent to spend a morning or an afternoon in the center sewing ripped clothes. Before the parent comes, have the children find the puppets, the dramatic play clothes, doll clothes, extra coats, and so on that need mending. Put all of these clothes in a neat pile. Get the needle and thread ready and pick a place where the parent will be comfortable and the children can watch the parent mend the clothes.

LANGUAGE GAMES

IT'S ME
Describe what a child is wearing. As soon as s/he recognizes him/herself, have him/her stand up and say, *"It's Me!"* Continue by describing each child. As you play describe several children more than one time to keep everyone's attention throughout the game.
EXTENSION:
During free play, have each child lay down on butcher paper. Trace around his/her body. Let each child paint clothes on him/herself.

TALK ABOUT
Discuss the different types of clothes that people wear in the various seasons. Have pictures available to stimulate discussion. Ask the children if they wear the same type of clothes as are in the pictures.

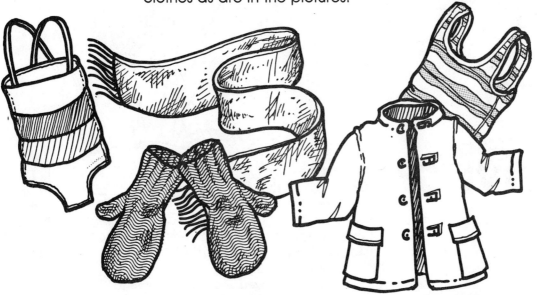

FELT BOARD FUN
Make a felt child and clothing for each season of the year. Put the child and the summer clothes on the felt board. Have the children name the clothes. Talk about when you wear the different clothes, such as the bathing suit for swimming, shorts for playing, etc. As you talk, have the children take turns dressing the felt child. Repeat the activity with appropriate clothes for the other seasons.

19

LANGUAGE GAMES

I'VE GOT A SECRET — Have five or six articles of clothing on a tray in front of you. Hold each one up and let the children call out its name. Now put the tray of clothes behind your back. Describe one of them. Let the children guess which one you are describing. When the children guess the item of clothes, hold it up and let them see it. Continue until the children have named all of the clothes.

LISTEN AND THINK — Have a bundle of various clothes. Hold up one piece of clothing and let the children identify it. Then ask, *"Do you wear a 'snowsuit' in the summer?"* The children softly call out, *"Yes"* or *"No"*. Continue with this manner using the remaining clothes.

ACTIVE GAMES

FOLLOWING DIRECTIONS — Get a large box and put it in the middle of the circle time area. Give directions to the children in relationship to the box. Instead of calling the children by name, describe what they are wearing.

> *"All of the children wearing shoes, come to the center of the circle, hold hands and walk around the box."*
>
> *"A boy wearing a blue shirt and brown pants, stand next to the box."*
>
> *"A child wearing red long socks, crawl inside the box."*
>
> *"A girl wearing a yellow blouse with brown buttons, hop around the box three times."*

Continue the game by mixing, matching, and varying the commands at as rapid a rate as the children can enjoy and understand.

ACTIVE GAMES

SINGING

Sing this song to the tune of *HERE WE GO 'ROUND THE MULBERRY BUSH.*

> *This is the way we put on snow pants,*
> *Put on snow pants, put on snow pants.*
> *This is the way we put on snow pants,*
> *All on a snowy morning.*
>
> *This is the way we put on our boots,*
>
> *This is the way we put on our coat,*
>
> *This is the way we put on our scarf,*
>
> *This is the way we put on our hat,*
>
> *This is the way we put on our mittens,*

Vary the verses of this song to coordinate with the season you are discussing.

BOOKS

EVE RICE — *NEW BLUE SHOES*
ESPHYR SLOBODKINA — *CAPS FOR SALE*
SHIGEO WATANABE — *HOW DO I PUT IT ON?*
GENE ZION — *NO ROSES FOR HARRY*

SELF CONCEPT

FIVE SENSES

FOR OPENERS

TAKE A PRETEND 'SENSE WALK'. HAVE ALL OF THE CHILDREN STAND UP. HAVE THEM BEGIN WALKING IN PLACE. START THE STORY.

"OH IT WAS A BEAUTIFUL DAY. THE WEATHER WAS WARM, THE WIND WAS BLOWING SLIGHTLY, AND TOMMY AND HIS MOTHER DECIDED TO GO FOR A WALK TO THE PARK. THEY PACKED A PICNIC LUNCH AND BEGAN TO WALK TO THE PARK. WHILE THEY WALKED THEY LOOKED (STOP AND LET THE CHILDREN POINT TO THEIR EYES.) FOR ALL OF THE ANIMALS, BIRDS, AND IN- SECTS. THE NEIGHBOR'S DOG CAME UP THE WALK TOWARD THEM. TOMMY STOPPED TO PET HER. (STOP AND LET THE CHILDREN TOUCH THEIR HANDS.) HER FUR WAS SO SOFT AND SILKY. ON THEY WENT TO THE PARK. OH NO! TOMMY AND HIS MOTHER HELD THEIR NOSES. (STOP AND LET THE CHILDREN DO THE SAME.) GUESS WHAT THEY SMELLED? YOU'RE RIGHT, THEY SMELLED A SKUNK. THEY STARTED WALKING FASTER TO GET AWAY FROM THAT SMELL. SOON THEY WERE FAR ENOUGH AWAY AND THEY COULD LET GO OF THEIR NOSES. THEY WERE A LITTLE OUT OF BREATH SINCE THEY HAD BEEN WALK- ING SO FAST. THEY WALKED A LITTLE SLOWER AND DID NOT TALK FOR A WHILE. THEY SIMPLY LISTENED FOR THE SOUNDS AROUND THEM. (STOP AND LET THE CHILDREN POINT TO THEIR EARS.) THEY COULD HEAR LOTS OF THINGS. WHAT DO YOU THINK WERE SOME OF THE SOUNDS THEY HEARD? (LET THE CHILDREN ANSWER.) FINALLY THEY REACHED THE PARK. IT HAD BEEN A LONG WALK AND THEY WERE HUNGRY. THEY SAT DOWN UNDER A BIG WILLOW TREE AND ENJOYED ALL OF THE TREATS IN THEIR LUNCH. (LET THE CHILDREN POINT TO THEIR TONGUES.) TOMMY PLAYED FOR AWHILE AND HIS MOTHER RESTED IN THE GREEN GRASS. AFTER AWHILE, TOMMY GOT TIRED. HE AND HIS MOM WALKED BACK HOME." REVERSE THE SE- QUENCE OF THE WALK BEGINNING WITH ALL OF THE SOUNDS TOMMY AND HIS MOM HEARD NEAR THE PARK. SEE HOW MANY OF THE DETAILS OF THE STORY THE CHILDREN CAN REMEMBER.

FINGERPLAYS

I STUCK MY HEAD IN A LITTLE SKUNK'S HOLE

I stuck my head in a little skunk's hole
And the little skunk said, "Why, bless my soul!
Take it out, take it out, take it out,
Remove it."

I didn't take it out and the little skunk said,
"You better take it out or you'll wish you had.
Take it out, take it out, take it out.
SHHHHHHHHHHH!" I removed it, TOO LATE!!

USE YOUR EYES

Use your eyes, use your eyes,
You can look and see;
If you have on brown shoes,
Come and stand by me.
 (Repeat this verse with the children,
 changing the various colors of clothing.)

USE YOUR EARS

Use your ears, use your ears,
Listen now and hear!
Use your ears, use your ears,
What kind of sound do you hear?
 (Have the children close their eyes.
 Make a sound with your body,
 such as a clap, a whistle, a snap
 of the fingers and so on. Let the
 children guess what sound you made.)

SOFT THINGS

I love soft things oh so much,
Soft things to feel,
Soft things to touch.
A cushioned chair,
A furry muff,
A baby's cheek,
A powder puff,
A bedtime kiss,
A gentle breeze,
My puppy's ear,
I love all of these.
 (After playing this game,
 talk about other things the
 children have that are soft.)

MY EYES

Here are my eyes,
One and two.
I give a wink.
So can you.
When they're open,
I can see the light.
When they're closed
It's dark like night.

SENSES

Eyes to see with,
Ears to hear with,
Nose to smell with,
Tongue to taste with,
Feet to run with,
Hands to touch with,
I'm a lucky child
Aren't you?

SELF CONCEPT

RECIPES

POPCORN

YOU'LL NEED

Kernels
Oil
Salt
Butter and cheese (optional)

TO MAKE: Follow the directions on the popcorn popper or make on the stove. Begin to pop the popcorn. As it is popping talk about the smell and the sound. At first there is no noise. Keep listening. Soon it gets louder and louder and then all of a sudden there is silence. What does that mean? Take the popcorn out of the popper. Let the children taste the snack without salt. Talk about how it tastes. Then add a little salt to the popcorn and taste again. Which do the children like better?

Sing the *POP CORN SONG* to the tune of *ROW, ROW, ROW YOUR BOAT.*

> *Pop, pop, pop your corn.*
> *Pop it big and white.*
> *Popping, popping, popping, popping*
> *Popping 'til it's right.*

FIELD TRIPS

● Visit a nearby florist. A floral shop has a beautiful aroma when you enter. This scent is the combination of many flowers and plants. During your visit to the shop, let the children have an opportunity to smell a variety of flowers. Talk about the smell. Some will probably smell good, others not as good, and still others will have very little scent. While you are there, have one of the florists create an arrangement for you to carry back to the school. Let the children watch as s/he puts in the base, the flowers, the greenery, and other decoration. When you return to school put the arrangement in a place for everyone to enjoy.

CLASSROOM VISITOR

● Have a nurse or doctor visit the class and show the children the instruments s/he uses when s/he examines a persons eyes, ears, nose, throat, and reflexes. Let the children examine the instruments with adult supervision.

LANGUAGE GAMES

LOOK WHAT'S HAPPENING

Get a toaster and try this food demonstration with the children. Have them all look at a piece of bread. Ask them to watch carefully as you put the piece of bread into the toaster. *"What is happening inside the toaster?"* When the bread pops up, *"What has happened to it?"* Let the children answer. Have the children cover their eyes. Now change the appearance of the toast by quickly putting butter on it. Have the children reopen their eyes, figure out what has changed and tell the rest of the children. Now have them cover their eyes again. Quickly put jam on the toast and let the children tell the group what has changed. Now cut the toast in half and discuss the change. Toast several more pieces of bread and enjoy them for a snack.

LOOK CAREFULLY

Give each child a magazine. Have them hunt for pictures which accent the *'five senses'*. Say to the children, *"Look through the magazine and find a picture of a person with blue eyes. When you have found one, point to it."* Let the children show their picture. *"OK, now find a picture of a furry animal."* Continue like this, having them find pictures and then talking about them.

LISTEN CAREFULLY

Have a horn, bell, alarm clock, whistle, and other objects that make noise. Take them out of a bag one at a time. Have the children identify the object. After they have named it, make a noise with the object. Then put all of the objects back into the bag. Have the children listen carefully while you turn around and play one of the objects. Turn back around and let the childen guess which object you just played. After they have guessed, bring it out and play it again. *"Did the sounds match?"* Do this with all of the objects in the bag.

25

LANGUAGE GAMES

TEXTURES
Have the children find parts of their clothes or bodies that have different textures. Start the game by saying, "*Look for something that you are wearing or a part of your body that is soft.*" Have the children discuss the things that they have found. Say, "*Now look for something that is rough.*" Again discuss. Then, "*What can you find that is sharp?*" Continue. For additional ideas about texture, see the unit on *TEXTURES*.

NEW FOODS
Read the story GREEN EGGS AND HAM by Dr. Seuss. As you are reading the story, talk with the children about eggs and ham. Then talk about '*green eggs and ham*'. When the story is over, ask them, "*Do you like to try new foods? Why? Why not? When was the last time that you tried a new food? What was it?*"

TASTING
Have the children stick out their tongue and touch it. Talk about the fact that tongues have '*taste buds*'. Have a variety of foods on a tray. First, let the children taste something '*salty*'. Then try '*sweet*' things, and then '*sour*'. As the children are eating the different foods, be sure to identify the taste that goes with the food. Talk about the part of the tongue which is responding to each taste.

CREATIVE THINKING
Ask the children, "*What are all of the things that we can do with our noses?*"

SMELLING
Have a tray of different foods that have a distinct smell (mustard, horseradish, peanut butter, onions). Let the children smell and name each item. Have the children cover their eyes. Take one food off of the tray. Walk around the circle and let each child smell the food. Put it back on the tray and then ask the children, "*What food did you just smell?*" After discussing that smell, play the game again with a different smell.

SMELLING SOAPS
Have a variety of soaps on a tray. Talk about what the different soaps are used for. Then let the children smell them. "*Which ones have a good smell? Which one has the best smell? Which soap smells the worst? Which one is the best to use when you are washing your hands?*"
At art, '*paint*' with bars of soap on black paper.

ACTIVE GAMES

TREASURE HUNT
Have a 'treasure hunt' around the room. Before circle time, hide pictures of all the senses. Tell the children that they are looking for these pictures and that when the music stops, they should return to their seats with the pictures that they have found. Play a record and let them search for a short time. When the music stops and the children have returned to their seats, let them describe what pictures they have found.

TONGUE EXERCISES
Lead the children in this activity.
- YUK — Stretch your tongue out as far as you can. Try to touch your nose or chin.
- GO UP TO THE ATTIC — Touch your tongue to the roof of your mouth.
- GO DOWN TO THE BASEMENT — Put your tongue as low inside your mouth as you can.
- TOUCH YOUR NOSE — Stretch your tongue as far as you can. Once again, try to touch your nose. Look around at the children. Talk for a minute about how some tongues are long, some are short, and so on. Maybe those who can touch their noses, can stand up and show the rest of the group.
- CURL UP — Keeping your tongue inside your mouth, see if you can curl up your tongue so that it points back to your throat.
- IN-OUT — Fast-fast, stick your tongue in and out of your mouth. Slow-slow, give your tongue a rest. Stick your tongue in and out as slowly as you can.
- AROUND THE BLOCK — Stretch your tongue out as far as you can. Then go all around your lips.

SMELLING WALK
Take a 'Smelling Walk' around the classroom. Before you begin the walk, talk about how the children think the floor, the tables, the walls, the shelves, the furniture, and so on might smell. "Do any of them have a smell?" Then let the children walk around the room and smell anything they would like to. When they return to the circle, talk about the different smells.

BOOKS

ALIKI — *MY FIVE SENSES*
BARBARA BRENNER — *FACES*
TANA HOBAN — *LOOK AGAIN*
AL PERKINS — *THE EAR BOOK*

SELF CONCEPT

27

SAFETY

FOR OPENERS

HAVE A PERSON FROM THE LOCAL FIRE DEPARTMENT VISIT YOUR CLASS. TALK ABOUT HOW FIRES START, WHAT TO DO IN CASE OF A FIRE, AND HOW TO CALL FOR EMERGENCY HELP WHEN YOU HAVE GOTTEN AWAY FROM THE FIRE. HAVE THE FIRE FIGHTER SHOW THE CHILDREN THE SAFEST AND FASTEST WAY OUT OF THEIR CLASSROOM. IN ADDITION, TAKE A WALK AROUND THE SCHOOL AND SHOW THE CHILDREN WHERE THE SPRINKLING SYSTEM IS AND / OR THE FIRE EXTINGUISHERS. IF THE FIREFIGHTER DROVE TO THE SCHOOL IN A FIRE TRUCK, HAVE HIM / HER SHOW THE CHILDREN SEVERAL OF THE SPECIAL FEATURES AND HOW THE BELLS AND SIRENS WORK.

FINGERPLAYS

LOOK BOTH WAYS
Stop at the corner,
Wait for the light,
Look to the left,
Look to the right.
If nothing is coming,
Then start and walk.
Go straight across the street,
Be careful and don't talk.

STOP, DROP, AND ROLL
Clothes on fire,
Don't get scared.
STOP!
DROP!
And ROLL!
            Dick Wilmes

SAFETY
Red says STOP.
Green says GO.
Yellow says CAUTION.
These are the colors you need to know.

SIRENS
When the siren blows,
It seems to say,
"Clear the street,
Get out of the way."
            Dick Wilmes

FINGERPLAYS

DAY AT THE BEACH
All the children laughing,
Having lots of fun,
Playing tag and racing,
In the summer sun.

Before we go in swimming,
One thing is for sure,
We put on our life vests,
And check that they're secure.

Water can be cooling,
Racing sure is fine,
But safety is important.
Keep thinking all of the time.
Dick Wilmes

MY WHEELS
Two wheels, three wheels on the ground,
My feet make the pedals go 'round and 'round.
Handle bars help me steer so straight,
Down the sidewalk, through the gate.
Dick Wilmes

RECIPES

As you eat the snack talk about safety

STOP SIGNS

YOU'LL NEED

Eight-sided crackers
Peanut butter
Natural red jam

TO MAKE: Spread a thin layer of
peanut butter on each cracker. Then
spread the red jam.

YIELD SIGNS

YOU'LL NEED

Triangle crackers
Yellow cheese

TO MAKE: Cut the yellow cheese into
triangles. Put the cheese onto the
crackers.

STOP AND GO LIGHTS

YOU'LL NEED

Rectangular crackers
Strawberries
Yellow cheese
Green olives

TO MAKE: Slice the strawberries,
cheese, and olives into circles. Let the
children put them on the crackers in
the right order.

CLASSROOM VISITOR

● Crossing guards or traffic police help children be safe each day. Ask the crossing guard near your school to visit the children. Have him/her wear his/her uniform.
Ask the guard to bring the safety signs and to explain the rules for safely crossing
the streets. Set up a pretend street and have the children practice crossing it safely
according to the crossing guard's directions.

LANGUAGE GAMES

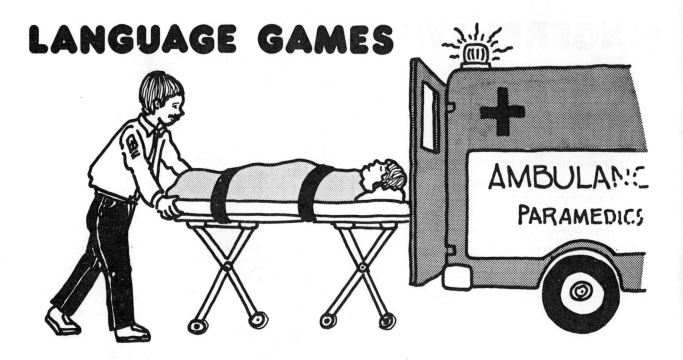

CREATIVE THINKING
Ask the children to think of all of the people that they know who help keep them safe. As the children think of people, have them tell the group aloud. Make a list of all of the people. Encourage the children to think beyond the police officer, firefighter, and doctor. Give them clues to help them remember moms and dads, paramedics, nurses, teachers, babysitters, etc.

EMERGENCY NUMBERS
Learn the *'Emergency Numbers'* for your area. Say them each day as a group. It will become like a chant. Talk about why it is so important to remember the *'Emergency Numbers'*.
EXTENSION:
Put play telephones in the Dramatic Play area and let the children practice dialing the *'Emergency Numbers'*.

PHONE NUMBERS
Have each child practice his/her own phone number. As children can remember, have them say their number aloud for the group. Then have them come up to the front and dial the number on a *'pretend'* phone.

WALKING SAFETY
Read this poem.
WALKING HOME
When I walk home from school today,
I'll walk the safe and careful way.
I'll look to the left — I'll look to the right.
Then cross the street when no car is in sight.
Talk with the children about how they take walks, who they walk with, where they go, and what time of day they are usually outside. Then talk about safety. Include all of the safety signs, such as the *'stop and go'* light, stop signs, and so on.
Make *'stop and go'* lights at art.

LANGUAGE GAMES

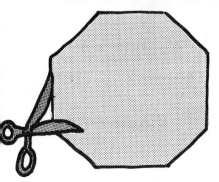  

FELT BOARD FUN
Make felt *'safety signs'*. Put them on the felt board. Play a guessing game, *"I'm thinking of a sign which means STOP."* Have a child come up take it off of the board, and carry it back to his/her place. After all of the signs are off the board, say different riddles. The child holding the sign should put it back on the felt board.

At art give each child a piece of construction paper that has been cut into the shape of a *'stop sign'* with the word STOP written on it. Have different types of beans available. Let the children glue the beans onto the letters.

HOME APPLIANCE SAFETY
Bring in several small home appliances, such as a mixer, blender, toaster, electric can opener, and so on. Supplement the real appliances with large pictures of additional appliances from magazines and newspapers. Talk about each appliance, what it is used for, and how to safely use it. Talk about accidents. Emphasize what the children would do if they or someone else had an accident with one of the appliances.

TOY SAFETY
Have a broken bike, wagon, big wheel, or other toy. Discuss all of the things which are unsafe about it. Talk about how you could make the toy safe again.

ACTIVE GAMES

FIRE DRILL
Walk out in the hall. Have the children tell you where all of the doors are which lead to the outside. Discuss which doors are closest and which are the farthest away. Talk about the best fire escape route and how to leave a building in case of fire. Then have the children *'role play'* a fire drill. As the children are safely walking outside, talk about the route that they are taking, how they are moving, and what they should do when they get away from the fire.

Have another *'fire drill'* from the classroom to outside of the building. This time pretend that the smoke is very thick. The children should crawl or scoot on their stomachs until they are clear of the *'smoke'*. Once again stress safety, how they are moving, and what to do when everyone is outside.

31

ACTIVE GAMES

SAFETY WALK   Make a 'safety trail' all around the center. Role play a 'safety walk'. "Stop and look at all of the safety signs that we've set up. Obey them. Watch out for cars. Do not talk to strangers that you meet along the way."

SINGING   Sing this safety song to the tune of *HERE WE GO 'ROUND THE MULBERRY BUSH.*

WE ARE SAFE

This is the way that we are safe,
We are safe, we are safe.
This is the way that we are safe,
Everyday of the year.

This is the way that we cross the street,
Look left then right, left then right.
This is the way we cross the street,
Look left then right for safety.

This is the way that we ride in the car,
Sit up straight, buckle your belt.
This is the way that we ride in the car,
Buckle your belt for safety.

This is the way that we phone for help,
Dial 911, dial 911.
This is the way we phone for help,
Dial 911 for safety.

Dick Wilmes

BOOKS

LEONARD KESSLER — *TALE OF TWO BICYCLES: SAFETY ON YOUR BIKE.*
VIRGINIA POULET — *BLUE BUG'S SAFETY BOOK*
JUDITH VIORST — *TRY IT AGAIN, SAM*

MY FEELINGS

FOR OPENERS

MAKE 'FEELING PUPPETS' BY GLUING LARGE PICTURES OF FACES ONTO PAINT STICKS. THESE FACES SHOULD CLEARLY DEPICT A VARIETY OF FEELINGS.

HOLD THE PUPPETS UP ONE AT A TIME. TELL THE CHILDREN THE NAME OF THE PUPPET, HOW S/HE IS FEELING, AND A SHORT STORY ABOUT WHY S/HE IS FEELING THAT WAY. FOR EXAMPLE, WHILE HOLDING THE "HAPPY" PUPPET YOU MIGHT SAY, "HI, FRIENDS. MY NAME IS JOKER. I AM FEELING SO HAPPY TODAY. I HAVE BEEN TELLING JOKES TO ALL OF MY FRIENDS THIS MORNING. WOULD YOU LIKE TO HEAR ONE? (TELL AN EASY JOKE TO THE GROUP.) GOOD-BYE, I HAVE TO GO AND TELL MORE FUNNY STORIES." ENCOURAGE THE CHILDREN TO RELATE INCIDENTS WHEN THEY HAVE BEEN VERY HAPPY. CONTINUE WITH THE OTHER FEELINGS.

FINGERPLAYS

FEELINGS
Smile when you're happy,
Cry when you are sad,
Giggle if it's funny,
Get angry if you're mad.
Dick Wilmes

WHO FEELS HAPPY
Who feels happy, who feels gay?
All who do, clap your hands this way.
Who feels happy, who feels gay?
All who do, nod their heads this way.
Who feels happy, who feels gay?
All who do, tap their shoulders this way.

I LOOKED INSIDE MY LOOKING GLASS
I looked inside my looking glass,
To see what I could see.
I guess I must be happy today,
Because that smiling face is ME.

STAND UP TALL
Stand up tall,
Hands in the air.
Now sit down
In your chair.
Clap your hands
And make a frown.
Smile and smile
Flop like a clown.

SING FOR JOY
I saw a child at play today,
Who did a funny thing.
Instead of feeling lonely
He began to sing.
Dick Wilmes

RECIPES

HOT ROLLS

YOU'LL NEED

1 pkg. of dry yeast
1 cup of warm water (not hot)
⅓ cup sugar (A little less if using honey)
⅓ cup of oil
3 cups of flour
A dash of salt

TO MAKE: Put the warm water in a bowl. Sprinkle the yeast on top of the water. Let the yeast settle into the water. Then mix all of the ingredients in a large bowl. Put the dough on a floured board to knead it. Let each of the children have the opportunity to knead the bread. (Bread baking, especially kneading, is a wonderful activity to work through emotions.) After kneading for about 10 minutes, put the ball of dough in a greased bowl. Cover the bowl and put in the sun or near heat.

Let it rise for about an hour or until doubled. Take the dough out of the bowl. "Punch" it down, knead for several more minutes and then divide into 12 to 15 pieces. Make each piece into a ball. Put on a cookie sheet or into muffin pans. Let rise again until doubled. Bake at 450 degrees for about 10-12 minutes.
from POLLY McNEIL

LANGUAGE GAMES

BODY TALK   Say to the children, *"Do you think that I'm happy when I make my body look like this?"* (The teacher makes the body look angry.) The children then answer, *"No!"* Say the sentence again but this time have a *'happy'* body. Do with 4 or 5 different feelings.

STUFFED TOYS   Have the children bring one of their favorite stuffed toys to class. Talk with the children about why they enjoy this particular stuffed toy. *"Does this toy make you happy? Does it make you less afraid? Do you talk to your toy? Does it talk back? What does it say?"* Continue.
    Have the children bring their stuffed toy to art. Give them a sheet of paper and have them trace around the toy. Paint the tracing with water colors.

LANGUAGE GAMES

HAPPY
FEELINGS

Talk specifically about the 'Happy' feeling. Then
tell short stories, such as, "It was a lovely Fall day and the
family decided to go to the zoo. This was Greg's first time at the
zoo." Then ask, "Do you think that Greg felt happy about the
trip?" If some children answer "No", ask them why and how
Greg might have felt. Then talk about all of the reasons that
Greg might have been happy about his trip to the zoo.
Continue the game by telling five or six more short, happy
stories.

SAD FEELINGS

Talk about the 'Sad' feeling. Have pictures of
different people who are looking sad. Think about and
discuss what could have made them sad. Encourage the
children to take cues from other things that are going on in
the picture.

ANGRY
FEELINGS

Discuss the 'Angry' feeling. Ask the children, "What makes
your mom angry?" Let them answer. Next ask them, "What
makes you angry?" Let them answer again. Then share with
them several things that make you angry.

FELT BOARD
FUN

Make a very simple large felt body without a 'face'.
Make several 'faces' that fit the body. Each 'face' should portray a different feeling. Put the body and all of the 'faces' on
the felt board. Tell a short story. Then let a child find a 'face'
that portrays how one of the characters in the story felt. Tell
several more stories.
EXTENSION:
Using the same felt board pieces described above, play
this game. Have a child stand up and portray an emotion
that matches one on the felt board. Have the remaining
children guess which feeling it is and then put the appropriate 'face' on the body.

IDENTIFYING
FEELINGS

Use the 'feeling faces' that you introduced in the OPENER
activity. Have a child come up and choose one of the
'faces'. Holding it so everyone can see, let the child name
the feeling and tell when s/he felt that same way. Then
have all of the children make their real faces look like the
feeling being discussed.

35

ACTIVE GAMES

FEELING HAPPY — Ask the children what their bodies do when they are happy. Some of the answers might be that they clap, jump up and down, smile, wiggle all over and so on. As the child says a way his/her body moves, let all of the children do it. Continue with other feelings.

SIMON SAYS — Play SIMON SAYS. *"Simon says, 'Walk around the circle being happy.' Simon says, 'Stop.' Simon says, 'Stomp around the circle being angry.' Simon says, 'Stop.' "* Your main aim is to concentrate on different feeling words, so avoid *'tricking'* the children.

DO AS I DO — Let the teacher lead this game. All of the children stand up. The teacher says, *"I'm feeling sad today."* Then she makes a sad face and body. The children do the same. Then, *"I'm feeling very angry today."* She makes her body look very angry and the children do the same. Continue playing the game for several more feelings.

MIRRORS — Have the children sit as pairs facing each other. Have one child make a *'feeling face'* at his/her partner. Let the other one guess what feeling it is. Now switch and do several more times.

SINGING — Sing *IF YOU'RE HAPPY AND YOU KNOW IT, CLAP YOUR HANDS.*

If you're happy and you know it, clap your hands.
If you're happy and you know it, clap your hands.
If you're happy and you know it,
Then your face will really show it.
If you're happy and you know it, clap your hands.

If you're sad and you know it, wipe your eyes.

If you're angry and you know it, stomp your feet.

BOOKS

CHILD'S WORLD — *HOW DO YOU FEEL?*
NORMA SIMON — *HOW DO YOU FEEL?*

FAMILIES

FOR OPENERS

READ THE POEM 'HOW MANY'

HOW MANY

HOW MANY PEOPLE LIVE AT YOUR HOUSE?

HOW MANY PEOPLE LIVE AT YOUR HOME?

ONE, MY MOTHER,

TWO, MY FATHER,

THREE, MY SISTER,

FOUR, MY BROTHER,

THERE'S ONE MORE, NOW LET ME SEE,

OH YES, OF COURSE,

IT MUST BE ME!

USE THIS AS A LEAD-IN TO DISCUSSING WHO LIVES IN EACH OF THE CHILDREN'S HOMES. LET EACH CHILD HAVE AN OPPORTUNITY TO TALK ABOUT HIS / HER FAMILY. ENCOURAGE THE CHILDREN TO NAME THEIR BROTHERS AND SISTERS, TELL WHAT THEY PLAY TOGETHER, IF THEY SHARE THEIR BEDROOM WITH ANYONE, AND SO ON.

FINGERPLAYS

GRANDMOTHER, GRANDFATHER

Grandmother, grandfather, do come in.
Grandmother, grandfather, how have you been?
Thanks for coming to visit awhile.
We can play some games, we can share a smile.

Grandmother, grandfather, as you leave today,
We're glad you came, glad you could stay.
Your visit has brought us a lot of joy.
Grandparents are special to each girl and boy.
                    Dick Wilmes

EVENING CHORES

The dishes need washing,
Mom and I are a team.
She washes, I wipe them,
Until they're all clean.

Dad and sister are helping,
They're sweeping the floors.
We all work together
When doing the chores.
                    Dick Wilmes

LET'S PRETEND

Let's pretend we're having fun
At a picnic everyone.
Then some picnic pets come 'round,
Birds that flutter to the ground,
Crickets who can jump so funny,
And a wiggly little bunny,
Butterflies on lazy wings,
Squirrels, ants, and lots of things!
Let's pretend that we are all
Picnic pets who've come to call.

37

RECIPES

ROLL-UPS

YOU'LL NEED

Bread
Your favorite cheeses and meats

TO MAKE: Roll out each piece of bread with a rolling pin. Put the cheeses and other ingredients on the bread. Roll up the sandwich.

Make these for snack and eat outside as if you were on a picnic.
DONNA DANE

LANGUAGE GAMES

TALK ABOUT
Have pictures of families doing activities. Give the pictures to the children. Have one child stand and hold up his/her picture so that everyone can see it. Let the children talk about what the family is doing. Continue until you have talked about all of the pictures.

CHORES
Talk about the chores that you do around the house. Ask the children what they do to help around their homes. Encourage them to be specific. If necessary prompt them by asking leading questions such as, *"Who makes their bed in the morning? Those who do, stand up."* Ask those who are standing if anyone helps them or if they do it by themselves. Ask them how big their bed is and how many blankets are on it. Continue the conversation by talking about other chores such as picking up toys, vacuuming, dusting, and so on.
EXTENSION:
Once you have discussed the household chores in general, ask each child to pick out the one s/he enjoys the most. Have him/her say the name of the job into the tape recorder. When everyone has had an opportunity to talk into the recorder, play it back and see if the children in the group can recognize whose voice is on the tape recorder. When someone recognizes who the child is, say the child's name and have the child stand up.

LANGUAGE GAMES

FAMILY FUN

Families have fun together. Start the conversation by telling some of the things that your family does for fun and relaxation. Let your events lead into stories told by the children. Encourage the children to talk about picnics, going to the movies, walks in the neighborhood, and other activities that you know are common in their families.

EXTENSION:
- Discuss picnics in more detail. Have a picnic basket filled with *'typical'* picnic goodies. Ask the children to guess what picnic items you have in the basket. As they guess the items, take them out and put them on the floor or picnic blanket in front of you. When all of the items are out of the basket, point to each object and have the children say the name of it aloud.
- Have the children cover their eyes. Take one of the picnic items away. After they have uncovered their eyes, see if they can remember which item is missing. When they know, they can quietly call it out. Put the item back. Have the children cover their eyes and repeat. Do this several more times.

FELT BOARD
FUN

'Mealtime' is often *'family time'*. Cut out pictures of all types of food. Back them with felt. Put the pictures on the felt board one at a time. Ask the children *"Does your family eat carrots?"* They can whisper, *"Yes"* or *"No."*

EXTENSION:
- Take this opportunity to discuss the four *'food groups'*. Have a picture of each food group. Using these pictures, talk about eating a *'balanced'* meal. Throughout the year continue talking about the foods that the children eat at snack and mealtime. Talk about what food group each food is in.
- Talk with the children about the *'mealtimes'* in their families. Discuss where they eat their meals, what they talk about at mealtimes, who eats together, and so on.
- At art give each child a paper plate. Put scraps of different types of paper in the middle of the table. Let the children collage a meal onto the plate.

S E L F C O N C E P T

ACTIVE GAMES

IDENTIFYING FOODS
Cut out between 15 and 20 different pictures of nutritional foods. With the children sitting in a circle, have one child walk around the outside and give each child a picture. When each child has a picture, go around the circle as fast as you can, letting each child hold up his/her picture and say what food s/he has. When each child has had a chance, collect all of the pictures. Choose another child to distribute pictures. Go around the circle again, this time trying to name the foods a little faster. Vary the activity by having the children identifying their foods very slowly.

FOLLOW THE LEADER
Discuss different ways that family members move, for example the baby 'crawls'. After you have identified all of the famly members and how they move, play 'Follow the Leader'. The 'leader' should vary the way s/he moves according to the discussion.

SINGING
Sing the following song to the tune of *HERE WE GO 'ROUND THE MULBERRY BUSH.*

This is the way we wash our clothes,
Wash our clothes, wash our clothes.
This is the way we wash our clothes,
All on a Monday morning,

This is the way we sweep the floor,
Sweep the floor, sweep the floor.
This is the way we sweep the floor,
All on a Tuesday morning,

Continue the song, using the chores that the children do at home. Do the actions to each chore as you sing the verse.

BOOKS

JOAN DRESCHER — *YOUR FAMILY, MY FAMILY*
MEREDITH TAX — *FAMILIES*

NUMBERS

FOR OPENERS

USING A PUPPET, HAVE IT CHALLENGE THE CHILDREN TO COUNT TO A SPECIFIC NUMBER. FOR EXAMPLE, HAVE THE PUPPET SAY, "HELP ME LEARN TO COUNT TO FIVE." LET THE CHILDREN COUNT. ONCE THEY HAVE COUNTED LET THE PUPPET COUNT TO THE SAME NUMBER FOR THE CHILDREN. DO THIS WITH ALL TEN NUMBERS. VARY THE WAY THE PUPPET CHALLENGES THE CHILDREN:

> "CAN YOU COUNT TO 7?"
> "I BET YOU ARE SMART ENOUGH TO COUNT TO 4."
> "LET ME HEAR YOU COUNT VERY QUIETLY TO 9."

FINGERPLAYS

FIVE LITTLE MONKEYS

Five little monkeys jumping on the bed.
One fell off and bumped his head.
Called for the doctor
And the doctor he said,
"No more monkeys jumping on the bed."

Four little monkeys jumping on the bed.
Etc.

Three little monkeys jumping on the bed.
Etc.

Two little monkeys jumping on the bed.
Etc.

One little monkey jumping on the bed.
One fell off and bumped his head.
Called for the doctor
And the doctor he said,
"No more monkeys jumping on the bed!"

I CAN EVEN COUNT SOME MORE

One, two, three, four,
I can even count some more.
Five, six, seven, eight,
All my fingers stand up straight.
Nine, ten are my thumb men.

ONE, TWO, BUCKLE MY SHOE

One, two buckle my shoe,
Three, four shut the door,
Five, six pick up sticks,
Seven, eight lay them straight,
Nine, ten a big fat hen.

FIVE FINGERS

Five fingers on this hand,
Five fingers on that.
One dear little nose,
One mouth that always goes.
Two cheeks so tiny and fat,
Two eyes, two ears,
And ten small toes.
That's the way a child grows.

BASIC CONCEPTS

FINGERPLAYS

FIVE LITTLE MONKEYS SWINGING FROM THE TREE

Five little monkeys swinging from the tree,
Teasing Mr. Alligator, "You can't catch me."
Along comes Mr. Alligator sneaky as can be.
SNAP!!!

Four little monkeys swinging from the tree,
Etc.

Three little monkeys swinging from the tree,
Etc.

Two little monkeys swinging from the tree,
Etc.

One little monkey swinging from the tree,
Etc.

No little monkeys swinging from the tree.

ONE, TWO, THREE

1, 2 how do you do?
1, 2, 3 clap with me.
1, 2, 3, 4 jump on the floor.
1, 2, 3, 4, 5 look bright and alive.
1, 2, 3, 4, 5, 6 pick up your sticks.
1, 2, 3, 4, 5, 6, 7 look up to heaven.
1, 2, 3, 4, 5, 6, 7, 8 draw a circle around your plate.
1, 2, 3, 4, 5, 6, 7, 8, 9 get the trucks in a line.
1, 2, 3, 4, 5, 6, 7, 8, 9, 10 let's do it over again.

RECIPES

NUMBERS

YOU'LL NEED

Sliced bread
Peanut butter
Raisins, carob chips or carrot circles.

TO MAKE: With peanut butter, write a number from 1-10 on each piece of bread. Give each child a piece of *'number'* bread and some raisins, chips or carrot circles. Let him/her trace over the peanut butter number with his/her topping. Before eating the *'Numbers'*, let each child say what number s/he has. Then enjoy the snack.

42

FIELD TRIPS

● Take a Number Walk. Walk around the vicinity of the school. Whenever you see a parked car in a safe area, stop and look at the license plate. Let the children read the numbers on the plate. As you see different plates you can talk about them in more detail. Do all of them have only numbers? What other kinds of symbols do some of the license plates have on them? What colors are the plates?

If you have parked your car in a safe place, let the children trace over the numbers on your plate with their fingers.

LANGUAGE GAMES

FELT BOARD FUN   Make ten rocket ships out of felt. As you put them on the board, have the children count. Then have a child come up and point to each one as the group counts them again. Challenge the children to count the rocket ships backwards. When they get to the last one they should say, *"Blast Off!"* and one of the children should fly the rocket ship around the room. Do this several times.

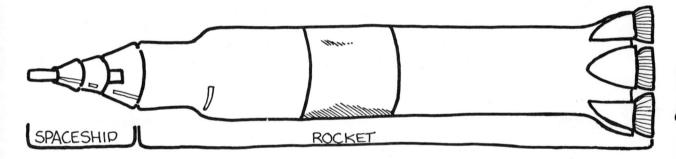

SPACESHIP   ROCKET

PING PONG COUNT   Have ten ping pong balls in front of you. Take a certain number out of the main pile and put them in a row. Have the children count as you touch each ball. Then have someone say how many there are in the group. Put the balls back into the main pile. Remove a different number of balls and count again. This activity can be continued as long as time and interest permit.

COUNTING BODY PARTS   Have the children find different parts of their body. As a group, count how many of each part you have. For example, a child might say *"fingernails"*. All of the group will find their fingernails and count them.

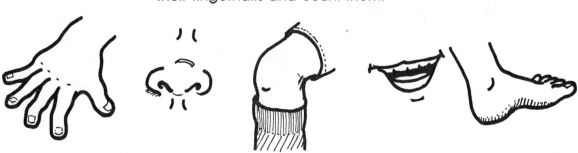

43

LANGUAGE GAMES

RECOGNIZING NUMERALS

Cut ten (or one for each child) 12" squares out of poster board. Write '1' on the first square, '2' on the second one, and so on up to '10'. Pass a number card to each child. Giving each child a turn, have him/her stand and hold the card for everyone to see. Have the group look at the number and say it aloud.

EXTENSION:

Using the ping pong balls from PING PONG COUNT, have a child lay his/her card in the middle of the circle and say the number. Then have another child put an appropriate amount of ping pong balls next to the card.

ACTIVE GAMES

FOLLOW THE LEADER

Go around the circle and let each child with 'dark hair' pick an action and do it however many times s/he chooses. (Limit it to ten times.) Then let him/her lead the group in doing it the same number of times. For example, s/he might choose to 'clap' five times. After s/he has done this, s/he then leads the entire group in 'clapping' five times. Continue with all of the 'dark haired' children. On another day, play the game again and let all of the 'light haired' children be leaders.

MOVING

Have the children stand up and move around the circle in the way that the teacher directs:

1-JUMP
2-STEPS
3-SLIDES
4-LEAPS
5-TIPTOES
6-TWIRLS
7-CRAWLS
8-GALLOPS
9-SKIPS
10-RUNS

Everyone counts as they do the actions.

ACTIVE GAMES

GO FISHING   Before circle time make thirty or more fish out of construction paper. Write a numeral on each one. Attach a paper clip to each and make a *'fishing pole'* for each child out of a dowel rod and a magnet tied to opposite ends of a string.

         Give each child several *'fish'* and let him/her put them in the *'lake'* . Now give the children *'fishing poles'* and let them *'fish'*. When all of the *'fish'* have been caught, bring them back to the circle. Identify the numerals written on each *'fish'*.

PARACHUTE PLAY   Have the children stand around the parachute (sheet) holding it with their fists up. Say a number, such as *"Six"*. The children should wave the parachute six times, counting as they move it. Say another number and wave the parachute again. Continue using other numbers and different holds.

BOOKS

ERIC CARLE — *ONE, TWO, THREE TO THE ZOO*
TANA HOBAN — *COUNT AND SEE*
DON NEDOBECK — *NEDOBECK'S NUMBERS BOOK*
MAURICE SENDAK — *ONE WAS JOHNNY*

SHAPES

FOR OPENERS

BEFORE CIRCLE TIME, MAKE A LARGE CIRCLE, SQUARE, AND TRIANGLE ALONG WITH FIVE CIRCLES, SQUARES, AND TRIANGLES OF ASSORTED SIZES.

PUT THE SMALLER SHAPES IN A BOX IN FRONT OF YOU. TELL THE CHILDREN THEY ARE GOING TO HELP YOU ORGANIZE THE SMALLER SHAPES. HOLD UP THE LARGE CIRCLE. ASK WHAT SHAPE IT IS. LAY IT DOWN. HOLD UP THE SQUARE AND NAME IT. HOLD UP THE LARGE TRIANGLE AND NAME IT. NOW HOLD UP ONE OF THE SMALLER SHAPES. ASK WHAT SHAPE IT IS. AS THE CHILDREN SAY IT, HAVE A CHILD LAY THE SHAPE ON TOP OF THE CORRESPONDING LARGE ONE. CONTINUE UNTIL ALL OF THE SHAPES HAVE BEEN SORTED.

FINGERPLAYS

DRAW A SQUARE

Draw a square, draw a square,
Shaped like a tile floor.
Draw a square, draw a square,
All with corners four.

DRAW A TRIANGLE

Draw a triangle, draw a triangle,
With corners three.
Draw a triangle, draw a triangle,
Draw it just for me.

DRAW A CIRCLE

Draw a circle, draw a circle,
Made very round.
Draw a circle, draw a circle,
No corners can be found.

HERE'S A BALL

Here's a ball.
Here's a ball.
Here's a great big ball I see.

Shall we count them?
Are you ready?
One, two three!

HERE'S A SUCKER

Here's a sucker
Big and fat.
Here's the stick
But you don't eat that.
                              Greg Wilmes

HERE'S A DONUT

Here's a donut
Big and fat.
Here's the hole
But you can't eat that.

RECIPES

SHAPE TREATS

Spread cheese or peanut butter on various shaped crackers.

Have cheese cut into circles, squares, and triangles

Have vegetable circles — cucumbers, carrots, zucchini, etc.

Cut fruit snacks — bananas, grapefruit wedges, apple slices, grapes.

FIELD TRIPS

● Take a Shape Walk through the school. Go very slowly through the halls of the school. As you walk, have the children look for things made in the shape of circles, squares, triangles, and rectangles. When someone sees a shape have him/her say "Stop." When the children have stopped the child should show the others where the shape is. When you find a shape that has a defined texture to it, have the children take the opportunity to rub over the shape with their hand.

LANGUAGE GAMES

TALK ABOUT SQUARES

Have a toy *'jack-in-the-box'*. Talk about the shape of the box. Look at all of the sides. Have the children say the shape of each side aloud. Enjoy this poem.

Jack-in-the-box,
Jack-in-the-box,
Will you come out?
Yes, I will!

IDENTIFYING SHAPES

Make different shapes out of construction paper before circle time. Hold up one shape at a time. If it is a square, the children say *"square"*. If it is another shape, the children should say, *"No"*. Play another day, emphasizing a different shape.

LANGUAGE GAMES

LOOK CAREFULLY   Have the children look around the room and find as many triangle shapes as they can. When a child finds a triangle, have him/her go to it, touch it, and say what the object is. Play again looking for squares, rectangles, or circles.

FELT BOARD FUN   Using the same color of felt, make several different size circles. Put them on the board. Have a child find the largest circle or the smallest one. Then have the children put the circles in order with the largest one first. When finished count the circles. Make this activity more difficult by adding different size circles.
EXTENSION:
Make different figures by using various circles. Start the thinking by making a snowman, a face, a ball decorated with smaller circles, a pile of ping pong balls or anything else that you can think of. After you have made one or two things, the children should be ready to think of their own ideas.

BODY SHAPES   Have the children look at their bodies. Looking carefully, ask them to find circles, then squares, and triangles.

ACTIVE GAMES

FOLLOWING ORDERS   Using tape, make a very large square in the circle time area. Have the children stand around the square. Now give commands, such as:
"Jump inside of the square."
"Hop up and down on both feet."
"Leap out of the square."
"Hold hands and walk around the square."
Continue on with seven or eight more commands.

MOVING   Make a large triangle shape out of a clothesline. Have the children move around the triangle in different ways — hop, tiptoe, walk, crawl, leap-frog, and so on. Have the children take turns being the leader.

ACTIVE GAMES

BALLOONS

Keep balloons in the air using swatters. Make a swatter for each child by bending a hanger into a kite shape. Cover the hanger with an old nylon. Tape the handle for safety. Blow up the balloons before circle time.

While passing out the balloons, talk about their shape. Let the children practice using their swatters and balloons. Then turn on some music and let them enjoy keeping the balloons in the air to the rhythm of favorite songs. When the music stops, the children should catch their balloons.

PASSING
THE SHAPES

At art have the children decorate a circle, square, or triangle with watercolors. Bring the shapes to circle time and pass them to music. When the music stops, the children should name the shape that they are holding. When the music resumes, the children should begin to pass the shapes again.

BOOKS

ED EMBERLEY — *WING ON A FLEA; A BOOK ABOUT SHAPES*
TANA HOBAN — *CIRCLES, TRIANGLES & SQUARES*
JOHN REISS — *SHAPES*

COLORS

FOR OPENERS

PLAY 'GO FISHING'. GIVE EACH CHILD A FISHING ROD WHICH YOU HAVE MADE FROM A STICK AND A SMALL MAGNET TIED TO OPPOSITE ENDS OF A STRING. CUT FISH OUT OF DIFFERENT COLORS OF CONSTRUCTION PAPER, WITH A PAPER CLIP FASTENED TO EACH FISH. PUT ALL OF THE FISH IN THE MIDDLE OF THE CIRCLE. HAVE THE CHILDREN STAND AROUND THE EDGE AND FISH. WHEN ALL OF THE FISH HAVE BEEN CAUGHT, THE CHILDREN SHOULD SIT BACK DOWN. TALK ABOUT THE COLORS OF THE FISH THAT THE CHILDREN HAVE CAUGHT. HAVE ALL OF THE CHILDREN HOLDING "RED" STAND UP. HAVE ALL OF THE CHILDREN HOLDING "BLUE" WAVE THEIR FISH. CONTINUE PLAYING THE GAME BY NAMING ALL OF THE COLORS OF FISH.

FINGERPLAYS

THE COLOR GARDEN

Red is the apple,
Up in the tree,
Hiding behind a green leaf,
Winking at me.

Blue is the little bird,
Sitting in her nest,
Who just caught a big brown worm,
And is now taking a rest.

Orange is the butterfly,
Floating near the brook.
Amid the purple violets,
Think I'll take a look.

Yellow is the sun up high,
Warming up the day.
With colors all around me,
I'm a lucky boy (girl) I'd say.

Black is the little animal,
Who isn't far away.
The stripe of white upon his back,
Tells me not to stay.
                    Dick Wilmes

RECIPES

Enjoy snacks which match the color of
the day.

YOU'LL NEED

Red — Tomatoes
Blue — Blueberry yogurt
Orange — Oranges
Yellow — Corn
Black — Raisins
Brown — Peanut Butter
White — Cauliflower
Green — Broccoli

FIELD TRIPS

● Visit a paint store. Have the attendant show the children the many shades of
each color of paint. This can be done by looking at the paint or by looking at the
different color charts s/he has. See if you can make prior arrangements with the
store for each child to have a swatch of colors showing the various shades of a certain color. If so, let the children each pick their favorite color and get a swatch of
the various shades from the paint attendant.

● Take a Color Walk. We oftentimes take color for granted. Take a walk with the
children to the nearest large sign, such as a billboard. Have them look at it closely,
searching for as many colors as they can find. Once they have looked at it for
several minutes, give each child the opportunity to share a specific color s/he
found. On the way back to the center look for more colors.

LANGUAGE GAMES

LOOK
CAREFULLY
Say a color. Have one child stand up. Have the other children look carefully at the child who is standing and name all
of the things that child is wearing that are the specified color.

LANGUAGE GAMES

SPINNER FUN

Make a spinner board. Cut a large circle out of white poster board. Divide it into eight sections. Color each section with one of the major colors. Fasten a pointer to the center of the circle with a brad.

Spin the pointer. When it stops, let the children who know the color say it. Now everyone say it together. Spin the pointer again. Have the children who know this color, name this second color. Continue until all of the colors have been identified.

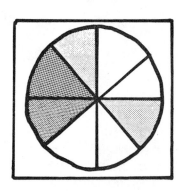 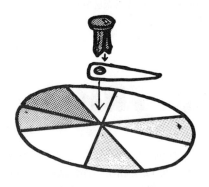

EXPLORING BLUE

Have blue food coloring and one glass of water. Drop several drops of the coloring into the glass. Let the children watch what happens to the water. Talk about what is happening. Add several more drops, what is happening now? Repeat several more times, talking about the change each time.

VARIATION:

Have several glasses of clear water. Put two drops of coloring into the first glass and talk about what is happening. Put four drops into the second glass. Note the difference between the first and second glasses. Put six drops into the third glass. Once again talk about the differences and similarities.

IDENTIFYING ORANGE

In the center of the circle have a bag full of orange objects — miniature cars, fruit, balloons, and other things from the classroom. Select the objects one at a time. Let a child say what the object is and tell its color. For example, the child might say something like, *"This is a car and it is orange."*

EXTENSION:

Play this game using other colors which you want to help the children identify.

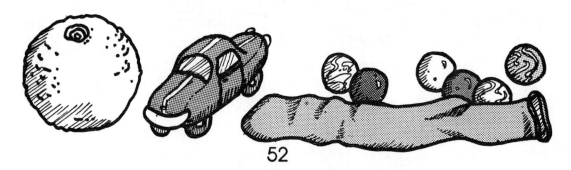

LANGUAGE GAMES

BROWN ANIMALS Have the children think about all of the animals that they have seen at the zoo. *"Which ones have brown fur?"* If they have difficulty remembering, give them several clues. After naming brown zoo animals, ask them, *"Who has a pet with brown fur?"* Let those children tell what type of pet that they have, the pet's name, and something interesting about their pet.

FELT BOARD FUN

• Make a white felt candle with a separate yellow flame for each child. Put the candles on the felt board. Count the candles with the children. Ask them what color the candles are. Then give each child a yellow flame. Ask the group what color the flame is. Go around the circle and let each child come to the felt board and light a candle. Count the flames as each child is lighting his/her candle.

• Make ten different colored crayons out of felt. Put them on the felt board. Have the children call out the color as you point to each crayon. Now play several games with the children.

    •• Have a child come to the board, take a specific color of crayon off the board and give it to you. Now have the children say the colors of the crayons which remain on the felt board. Put the crayon back on the board. Have a child take a specific color crayon off the board and play again.

    •• Put all of the crayons in a row. Have a child come up and point to the *'second crayon'* and name its color. Do this activity several times using different position words.

• Make a large bare tree out of dark felt and a variety of leaves out of different shades of green felt. Put the bare tree on the felt board. Ask the children what grows on trees. As you talk about the different things that grow on trees, hang the leaves. When you have thought about everything that hangs from trees, talk about the different shades of green leaves.

YELLOW RIDDLES Say riddles about yellow things — sun, bananas, lemons, dandelions, caution lights, and other things. Give the children clues about each thing and let them identify it.

LANGUAGE GAMES

BLACK ITEMS   Gather black items such as a chalkboard eraser, pencil, car, crayon, hat, animal, bottle of black ink, construction paper, and others. Put all of the items into a pillow case. Take them out one at a time and have the children call out what the item is and its color. For example, they might say, *"A black crayon."* Continue pulling items out until the bag is empty and all of the black items are on the floor in front of you.
EXTENSION:
    Have the children cover their eyes. Take one of the objects away. Have the children uncover their eyes and see if they know what object is missing. Put the object back and repeat the game several more times.

ACTIVE GAMES

ARM DANCING   Do arm dancing with crayons on a long sheet of newsprint. Get two crayons for each child. (It is better if the paper wrapping has been taken off of the crayons.) Pick several different records that have various tempos. At circle time, roll out the sheet of newsprint on the floor. Have the children sit around the newsprint leaving room between each other. Let each child pick two colors. When the music starts, the children should begin to color with their crayons to the tempo of the music. After several minutes, change the music and now let the children *'dance'* to the new tempo. Continue until you have played three or four different selections. When the *'dancing'* is over, talk about all of the colors in the mural and then hang it for everyone to enjoy.

PASSING ORANGES   Have one or two oranges. When the music begins, start passing the oranges around the circle. When the music stops, the children who have the oranges should stand up and turn around; then they can begin the game when the music starts up again.

ACTIVE GAMES

DANCING   Dance to favorite music using colored streamers.
EXTENSION:
    While the children are dancing, call out, *'Those with blue streamers freeze. Those with yellow streamers wave them up high."* Continue giving a variety of directions.

LETTER CARRIERS   Have colored pieces of construction paper cut in the shape of rectangles to represent pieces of mail. Choose one child to be the letter carrier. Have him/her go around the circle and deliver a *'letter'* to each child. When all of the *'letters'* have been delivered, let each child stand up and tell what color *'letter'* s/he received. Collect all of the *'letters'*, redistribute them, and let the children identify the color of the second *'letter'* s/he received.

BALLOON BOUNCE   Blow up a balloon for each child. As you pass the balloons out, talk about the colors. Ask the children if they have ever decorated their homes with balloons. What color of balloons did they use? After the discussion, play some music and have the children try to keep the balloons up in the air using their hands. If the balloons fall to the floor, have the children pick them up and start over again.

SINGING   Chant the song *WHAT ARE YOU WEARING*

    TEACHER: *Blue, blue, blue, blue*
                      Who is wearing blue today?
                      Blue, blue, blue, blue,
                      Who is wearing blue?

    CHILDREN: (Those who are wearing blue stand up and say):
                      I am wearing blue today.
                      Look at me and you'll say,
                      Blue, blue, blue, blue,
                      I am wearing blue.

BOOKS

TANA HOBAN — *IS IT RED?*
BILL MARTIN — *BROWN BEAR, BROWN BEAR, WHAT DO YOU SEE?*
JOHN REISS — *COLORS*

ALPHABET

FOR OPENERS

AS THE CHILDREN ARE COMING TO THE CIRCLE AREA, BEGIN SINGING THE ALPHABET SONG. ENCOURAGE THE CHILDREN TO JOIN IN AS THEY ARRIVE.

VARIATION: SING THE SONG SLOWLY, HOLDING UP EACH LETTER AS IT IS SUNG.

SING IT AT REGULAR SPEED AND THEN CHALLENGE THE GROUP TO SING IT FASTER, BUT SO YOU CAN STILL UNDERSTAND ALL OF THE LETTERS BEING SAID.

RECIPES

A B C SOUP

YOU'LL NEED

6 cups of water
1 quart tomato juice
1 medium onion
2 carrots
2 stalks of celery
Other vegetables you'd like
2 bay leaves
2 allspice balls
Salt and pepper to taste
½ cup of A B C noodles

TO MAKE: Simmer the tomato juice, water, and seasonings. Fix the remaining vegetables and add to the liquid. Simmer for about 20 minutes. Add the noodles and cook for about 15 minutes longer.
from COME AND GET IT
by Kathleen Baxter

FIELD TRIPS

● Visit your local library. Call ahead for an appointment. At this time also request that the children be able to examine the books written in braille. These books will be new to many of the children. The librarian should talk about these special books, who they are for, how they work, and how to care for them. If possible have the librarian help the children feel the letters written in braille.

LANGUAGE GAMES

FELT BOARD FUN
● Make all of the letters in the alphabet out of felt. Put a letter on the felt board. If any child knows the letter name, have him/her call it out. Continue through the entire alphabet.
● Pass out all of the felt capital letters. Say *"Who has an F? Please put it on the felt board."* Pick another letter and have that child put it on the felt board. Assist children who need help recognizing their letters. Continue until all of the letters are on the board.

EXTENSION:
When all of the letters are on the board, help the children put them in alphabetical order. Say *"A"*. Have someone find the A and put it first in the row. Say *"B"*. Have someone put it next to the A. Continue through Z. Sing the *ALPHABET SONG,* pointing to the letters as the children sing.

57

LANGUAGE GAMES

FIRST LETTER
Have a set of capital letter alphabet cards. Hold up a letter and say its name. If a child's name begins with that letter, have the child stand up. Some children will recognize the letter by themselves, others will need assistance. Continue holding up different capital letters until all of the children are standing.

RECOGNIZING
LETTERS
Before circle time, find some ads in magazines and newspapers which have large recognizable letters, such as McDonalds, K-Mart, Zayre, Burger King, etc. Cut out the ads.
  Hold the ads up one at a time. See If any of the children can recognize what is being advertised. Talk about the letters in the ad.
EXTENSION:
  After discussing the letters, read the ad to the children. Talk about what the ad says.

NAME
Write each child's name in large letters on individual pieces of lightweight cardboard. Have them each decorate their card at art. Bring the cards to circle time.
  Hold up each card. As a child recognizes his/her name, the child should stand up. As the child stands, clap for him/her and give the child the name card.
EXTENSION:
  When each child has a card, play this game. Point to a child and have him/her hold up the name card. Point to one of the letters on the name card and have the group call out the name of the letter.

LOOK
CAREFULLY
Put a bunch of letters in the middle of the circle so that everyone can see them. Say, *"I am looking for an 'A'. Who sees one?"* Have a child who sees the letter get it and bring it to you. Continue until all of the letters have been picked up.

ACTIVE GAMES

PASS THE LETTER   Have a complete set of alphabet letters. Give several to
each child. Have them each select one and leave the remainder in a pile in front of them. Begin playing some
music. While the music is playing, have the children pass
the letters around the circle. When the music stops, have
each child hold up his/her letter and say which letter it is.
Now have them choose another letter from their pile and
begin passing them to the music again. Continue on to
give all of the children practice in recognizing letters.

MAIL THE LETTER   Before circle time, put one letter in each of 26
envelopes. (Do not seal them.) Put all of the envelopes in a
bag. At circle time let one of the children be a letter carrier
and deliver an envelope to each child. One at a time have
the children open their envelope and hold up the letter
which is inside. The group whispers the name of the letter
each child is holding up. Have the children put the letters
back in their envelopes and collect all of them. Play once
or twice more, giving other children the opportunity to be
the letter carrier.

BOOKS

TERRY BERGER — *BEN'S ABC DAY*
KATE GREENAWAY — *A-APPLE PIE*
TANA HOBAN — *A, B, SEE*
ARNOLD LOBEL — *ON MARKET STREET*

BASIC CONCEPTS

TEXTURES

FOR OPENERS

GET SMALL PAPER BAGS AND MAKE A 'FEELING BAG' FOR EACH CHILD. PUT A DIFFERENT TEXTURE IN EACH BAG — SANDPAPER, VARIOUS FABRICS, SPONGE, CORRUGATED PAPER, TEXTURED WALLPAPER, AND SO FORTH. CLOSE THE BAG.

AT CIRCLE TIME, GIVE THE CHILDREN EACH A BAG. HAVE THEM PUT THEIR HAND IN THE BAG AND FEEL THE TEXTURE. WHEN A CHILD THINKS SHE / HE KNOWS WHAT IS IN THE BAG, HAVE HIM / HER CLOSE IT. WHEN ALL OF THE BAGS ARE CLOSED, LET EACH CHILD TELL WHAT IS IN THE BAG. AFTER GUESSING, OPEN THE BAG AND PULL OUT THE TEXTURE. PASS THE DIFFERENT TEXTURES AROUND THE CIRCLE. DISCUSS HOW THEY FEEL.

FINGERPLAYS

OCEAN SHELL

I found a great big shell one day,
Upon the ocean floor.
I held it close up to my ear,
And heard the ocean roar!

I found a tiny little shell,
Upon the ocean sand.
The waves had worn it nice and smooth,
It felt nice in my hand.

SOFT KITTY

Soft kitty, warm kitty,
Little ball of fur.
Lazy kitty, pretty kitty,
"Purr, purr, purr."

TOUCH

I love soft things so very much,
Soft things to feel,
Soft things to touch.
A cushioned chair,
A furry muff,
A baby's cheek,
A powder puff,
A bedtime kiss,
A gentle breeze,
A puppy's ear,
I love all of these.

FUZZY WUZZY CATERPILLAR

Fuzzy wuzzy caterpillar
Into a corner will creep.
He'll spin himself a blanket,
And then go fast to sleep.

Fuzzy wuzzy caterpillar,
Wakes up by and by,
To find with wings of beauty,
He's changed to a butterfly.

60

RECIPES

TEXTURES

Use these recipes in two ways:
1. Let the children feel the ingredients before they make the snack.
2. Before the children actually swallow the food, ask them to think about how it feels in their mouths. Talk about the texture of the food.

HOMEMADE NOODLES
YOU'LL NEED

1 beaten egg
2 T. milk
½ t. salt
1 cup flour

TO MAKE: Combine the first three ingredients. Add enough flour to make a stiff dough. Roll very thin on a floured surface. Let the mixture stand for about 20 minutes. Roll up loosely, cut slices ¼ inch wide, unroll, spread out and let dry for several hours. Dried noodles can be stored in a sealed container until needed.

To cook, drop the noodles into boiling water or soup and cook uncovered about 10 minutes.

Makes about 3 cups of cooked noodles.

PEANUT BUTTER BALLS
YOU'LL NEED

4 oz. peanut butter
1 T. honey
½ cup of non-fat dry milk

TO MAKE: Mix all of the above ingredients. If necessary, add more dry milk. Let the children enjoy making balls out of the mixture. Refrigerate.

FRUIT POPSICLES
YOU'LL NEED

Fruit juice
Small paper cups
Popsicle sticks

TO MAKE: Pour the juice into cups. Put all of the cups into the freezer. When they are partially hardened, stick the popsicle sticks in them and leave them in the freezer to continue to harden. When totally hardened, peel the cup away and enjoy on a warm day.

VEGETABLE PACK
YOU'LL NEED

Celery
Carrots
Spinach
Cauliflower
Mushrooms
Other fresh vegetables

TO MAKE: Pick a variety of vegetables each of which have a different texture. Clean the vegetables. Talk about the texture as you scrub them. Eat them.

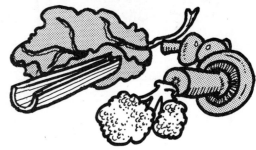

BASIC CONCEPTS

FIELD TRIPS

● Walk to the park and examine the trees. Feel all of the different parts of the tree and talk about how they feel. Feel the bark on the trunk and on the branches, touch the leaves, the seeds, and the buds. Are there any thorns or other prickly shoots growing on the tree. Use words such as smooth, bumpy, rough, prickly, and so on to describe the textures you touch on the trees.

● Go to a nearby parking lot or concrete-surfaced area such as a basketball court. Walk slowly around the area, touching the surface in different parts. Do all areas of the lot feel the same? Did anyone feel a different texture? What was it?

● Take a Texture Walk to an open field. Walk slowly. The ground changes often. Give the children time to reach down and feel the ground in several different places. Once again try to label the ways the ground feels. Does the field feel the same as the parking lot? How is it different? The same?

LANGUAGE GAMES

SIT AROUND
A TEXTURE

Each day when the children come to circle time, have a different texture on the floor for them to sit around. Use textures such as a blanket, sheet, bedspread, paper tablecloth, or a large piece of carpeting. Talk about how the texture feels.

TEXTURE TOUCH   Collect materials with different textures, such as satin, wool, sandpaper, aluminum foil, and a sponge. Cut each into enough pieces so that each child will have one of each. Pass out pieces of the first texture. Let the children feel it. How does it feel? Collect the first texture, pass out another and talk about it. Continue until all of the textures have been discussed.

LANGUAGE GAMES

FEEL AND GUESS   Gather some common objects, such as crayons, pencils, sponges, cotton balls, rocks, small blocks, leaves, combs, paint brushes, and toy cars. Hold up each object and let the children call out its name. Go over to a child. Have the child cover his/her eyes. Give the child an object. Ask him/her to feel the object and try to figure out what it is. When s/he thinks that s/he knows, have him/her say what it is. Have the child open his/her eyes and see if the guess was correct. Go to another child and repeat.

ACTIVE GAMES

WALK AND FEEL   Have the children walk around the room feeling the different surfaces of the classroom walls. *"How many different textures are there? Wood, brick, cement block, wallpaper? What else?"*
EXTENSION:
Another time have them crawl and feel the different textures of the floor. Try this again by touching the textures on the furniture.

TEXTURE WALK   Have a TEXTURE WALK. Get approximately 10 large plastic dish tubs. Gather a different texture to put in each tub — styrofoam pieces, rubber bands, sand, macaroni noodles, rice, flour, dirt, string, cooked spaghetti, sandpaper, water. After you have put a texture in each tub, arrange them in a straight line. Have the children take their shoes and socks off and walk from tub to tub squishing their feet in the contents. (If a child needs help going from tub to tub, hold hands. If a child is hesitant about going on the walk, suggest that s/he walk alongside of the tubs and pretend to put her/his feet in each tub.) When everyone has experienced the TEXTURE WALK, talk about the different textures:
Which one did you like the best?/Least?
Which one tickled?/Itched?
Which one was the smoothest?/Roughest?
Did any stick to your feet?

ACTIVE GAMES

BEAN BAG FUN — Make or buy bean bags with different textured cloths. Play a variety of bean bag games:

- PASS THE BEAN BAG: The children should be sitting in a circle. Have one bean bag. Start some music. The children should begin passing the bean bag around the circle. When the music stops, the child holding the bean bag must stand up. When the music starts again the child should sit down and start passing the bean bag around the circle.
- BALANCE THE BEAN BAG: Give each child a bean bag. Have them put the bean bag on different parts of their bodies and walk around the circle trying to keep the bean bag balanced. Start with easier places such as the child's hand. Progress to more difficult places such as the head and shoulders.
- MARCH, MARCH, MARCH: Once the children know how to balance the bean bags on their heads, have a make-believe band. Let each child balance a bean bag as they pretend to play an instrument. This is fun around a holiday.

BOOKS

VIRGINIA JENSEN — *WHAT'S THAT?*
DOROTHY KUNHARDT — *PAT THE BUNNY*

FARM ANIMALS

FOR OPENERS

HAVE PICTURES OF A VARIETY OF FARM ANIMALS. DISPLAY THEM ON A LARGE PIECE OF STYROFOAM BOARD THAT HAS BEEN CUT INTO THE SHAPE OF A BARN. POINT TO EACH ANIMAL AND HAVE THE CHILDREN CALL OUT ITS NAME. ONCE THEY KNOW THE ANIMAL NAMES, PLAY A RIDDLE GAME. DESCRIBE THE ANIMALS ONE AT A TIME. LET THE CHILDREN GUESS WHICH ONE YOU ARE TALKING ABOUT. WHEN THE CHILD GUESSES, HAVE HIM / HER COME UP AND TAKE THE APPROPRIATE ANIMAL OUT OF THE BARN TO THE PASTURE. WHEN ALL OF THE ANIMALS ARE IN THE PASTURE SAY, "IT IS TIME FOR THE ANIMALS TO BE PUT IN THE BARN. THE PERSON HOLDING THE SHEEP BRING IT BACK TO THE BARN. THE PERSON HOLDING THE PIG, BRING IT BACK." CONTINUE UNTIL ALL OF THE ANIMALS ARE BACK IN THE BARN.

FINGERPLAYS

THE COWS

Here is the barn so big, don't you see?
In walk the cows, one, two, three.
Soon there'll be milk for you and for me.

MR. DUCK AND MR. TURKEY

Mr. Duck went out to walk
One day in pleasant weather.
He met Mr. Turkey on the way
And so they talked together.
"Gobble, gobble, gobble."
"Quack, quack, quack, quack, quack."
"See you soon, Good bye!" they said.
And then Mr. Duck walked back.

THIS LITTLE PIG

This little pig went to market,
This little pig stayed home,
This little pig had roast beef,
This little pig had none,
This little pig cried, "Wee, wee, wee,
I can't find my way home."

TEN FLUFFY CHICKENS

Five eggs and five eggs,
That makes ten.
Sitting on top is the Mother Hen.
Crackle, crackle, crackle,
What do I see?
Ten fluffy chickens,
As yellow as can be.

THE LAMBS

This is the meadow, where all the day
Ten little lambs are all at play.
These are the big shears to shear the old sheep.
The dear little lambs, their soft wool may keep.

ANIMALS

RECIPES

Enjoy eating snacks along with the farm animals:

Chicken — Corn
Cow — Corn
Pig — Vegetables
Horse — Apples and carrots
Sheep — Corn
Turkey — Nuts and berries

FIELD TRIPS

● Visit a farm which primarily raises animals. If you are visiting a dairy farm, try to schedule the visit at milking time. If this cannot be coordinated, make arrangements for the farmer to show the children how the milking machines operate. While walking around the farm note the barns where the animals live, what they are fed, and the machinery that is used to help the farmer do the daily chores.

LANGUAGE GAMES

ANIMAL TALK

Play a word matching game about farm animals and the noises they make.

Say the name of the animal, such as *'duck'* and have the children say what type of sound that animal makes, such as *"Quack, quack, quack"*. Continue playing the game using these and other animals.

CHICKEN: *Cluck, cluck, cluck*
COW: *Moooo*
PIG: *Oink, Oink,* with some squeals and grunts
HORSE: *Whinny, whinny*
SHEEP: *Baah, baah, baaaaah*

CREATIVE
THINKING

Ask *"Who has ever seen cows? Where were they? What were they doing?"*
Once the children have had the opportunity to talk about cows, ask them, *"What do cows think about as they eat? Do you think that cows talk to each other? How? What do they say?"*

EXTENSION:

Make butter with the children. Put one-half pint of whipping cream into a large jar. Have the children sit in a circle and roll the large jar quickly back and forth among themselves. When butter has formed, let each child spread some on a cracker and eat it. When everyone has tasted it, add a little salt to the remaining butter. Try it again. Do the children like the butter with or without salt?

LANGUAGE GAMES

FELT BOARD FUN

• Make a set of five cows which range in size from large to small. Put them on the felt board. Ask a child to come up and point to the largest cow. *"Let's think of a name for this cow."* Once the cow has a name, ask a child to come up and touch the smallest cow. *"Who can name this cow?"* Then have a child come up and arrange all five cows from the largest to the smallest. Review the names of the largest and smallest cows. Give names to the others. Ask if these five cows could be a family. Which one is the dad, the mom, and the calves?

• Make ten identical chickens. Play a variety of games:

•• Count the chickens forward and backward.

•• Have a child come up to the board and take a certain number of chickens off. Have the group count as the child removes the chickens and then count how many are left on the board

•• Put the chickens in a row. Ask a child to come up and *"Point to the second chicken."* Continue through all of the ordinal numbers.

DUCK TALK

Many of the children have probably fed ducks or at least seen them. Talk about how they sound, walk, look, etc. Let the children pretend that they are ducks. Have them pair off, look at each other and talk in *'duck talk'* to each other. Have one child say something in *'duck talk'* and have his/her partner answer in *'regular talk'.* Switch.

PIG PUPPETS

At art make pig puppets out of paper bags. Have the children bring their puppets to circle time. Let each child stand up and tell the others what their pig's name is, where s/he lives, and what games s/he like to play.

ACTIVE GAMES

PARACHUTE PLAY Using your parachute (sheet) as a pretend 'farmyard', have the 'animals' come in for feeding. Divide the children into small groups of different 'farm animals'. First come the 'cows'. Have the children get down on 'all fours' and move around the 'farmyard' in single file as cows would. Next come the 'ducks' waddling around in a line. The 'chickens' cluster together as they come in to feed. When all of the 'farm animals' have gathered, eat snack.

DUCK, DUCK GOOSE Ducks and geese are found on most farms. Sometimes these animals are pets, other times not. Enjoy playing this longtime favorite with the children.

TAPE THE FLEECE ON THE SHEEP Cut out a large silhouette of a sheep. Tack it low on a bulletin board. Give each child several fluffy cotton balls with double-faced tape on one side. Taking turns, have each child cover his/her eyes and tape the cotton onto the sheep. Soon the sheep will be full of warm fluffy 'wool'.

68

ACTIVE GAMES

SINGING

• Chant the active poem, *"FIVE LITTLE DUCKS"*.

Five little ducks that I once knew,
Fat one, skinny one, tall ones two.
But the one little duck,
With the feather on his back,
He led the others with a "Quack, quack,quack,
Quack, quack, quack."

Down to the river they would go,
Wibble, wobble, wibble, wobble to and fro.
But the one little duck,
With the feather on his back,
He led the others with a "Quack, quack, quack,
Quack, quack, quack".

Up from the river they would come,
Ho, ho, ho, hum, hum, hum.
But the one little duck,
With the feather on his back,
He led the others with a "Quack, quack, quack,
Quack, quack, quack".

(Once the children know the words, pretend to be little ducks and move as you chant the poem.)

• Enjoy the song, *"DID YOU FEED MY COW?"*

Did you feed my cow?
Yes ma'am!
Will you tell me how?
Yes ma'am!
Oh, what did you give her?
Corn and hay.
Oh, what did you give her?
Corn and hay.

Did you milk her good?
Yes ma'am!
Did you do it like you should?
Yes ma'am!
Oh, how did you milk her?
Swish, swish, swish!
Oh, how did you milk her?
Swish, swish, swish!

• Enjoy singing *"OLD McDONALD HAD A FARM"* and playing the game THE FARMER IN THE DELL.

BOOKS

PHOEBE & JUDI DUNN — *ANIMALS OF BUTTERCUP FARM*
CHIYOKO NAKATANI — *MY DAY ON THE FARM*
FEODOR ROJANKOWSKY — *ANIMALS ON THE FARM*

ANIMALS

69

PETS

FOR OPENERS

PLAY 'TELEPHONE' WITH THE GROUP. GIVE EACH CHILD A TOILET PAPER ROLL TO TALK THROUGH. BEGIN THE GAME BY TALKING TO THE CHILD NEXT TO YOU. SAY, "A DOG SAYS, 'RUFF, RUFF, RUFF.' " THE CHILD THEN REPEATS IT TO THE NEXT CHILD. ALWAYS USING THE TOILET PAPER ROLLS TO TALK THROUGH, CONTINUE AROUND THE CIRCLE. THE LAST CHILD SAYS THE MESSAGE ALOUD. CONTINUE THE GAME USING SOUNDS OF OTHER PETS THE CHILDREN HAVE. (A CAT SAYS, "MEOW, MEOW, MEOW." A GOLDFISH MAKES A QUIET HISSING SOUND. A BIRD SAYS "TWEET, TWEET, TWEET." A HAMPSTER MAKES A SQUEAKING NOISE. A FROG GOES "RIBBIT, RIBBIT,RIBBIT.")

FINGERPLAYS

SOFT KITTY

Soft kitty, warm kitty,
Little ball of fur,
Lazy kitty, pretty kitty,
"Purr, purr, purr!"

THE PUPPY

Call the puppy,
Give him some milk,
Brush his coat
'Til it shines like silk,

Call the dog
And give him a bone.
Take him for a walk,
Then bring him home.

MY PETS

I have five pets
That I'd like you to meet.
They live with me on Mulberry Street.

This is my chicken,
The smallest of all.
He comes running whenever I call.

This is my duckling,
He says, "Quack, quack, quack"
As he shakes all the water off of his back.

Here is my rabbit, he runs from his pen.
Then I must catch him and put him back in again.

This is my kitten.
Her fur is black and white.
She wants to sleep on my pillow each night.

Here is my puppy who has lots of fun.
He chases the others and makes them all run.

(Talk about who has which of the pets mentioned
in the rhyme. Does anyone have all five pets?)

FRED AND HIS FISH

Fred had a fish bowl.
In it was a fish,
Swimming around
With a swish, swish, swish.

Fred said, "I know what I will do.
I'll buy another fish and that will make _____."

ANIMALS

RECIPES

Eat snacks that the pets would like:
Cat — Milk
Hamster — Bread and Vegetables
Dog — Meat
Bird — Sunflower seeds

FIELD TRIPS

● Make an appointment to visit the local pet store. Have the clerk show you some of the types of animals people have for pets. In addition have him/her explain how to care for and feed the different pets.

CLASSROOM VISITOR

● Have four or five parents bring their family pets to the center. When arranging this, try to have a variety of pets represented. Have several dogs such as a large one and small one or one with long hair and one with short, a couple of different colored cats, a bird, a goldfish, and a small mammal such as a hamster or gerbil. Do any of the families have peculiar kinds of pets? What?

LANGUAGE GAMES

LISTEN CAREFULLY The children should sit in a circle. One child is selected to be the *Mother Cat*. After *Mother Cat* has left the room, choose several other children to be *kittens*. All of the children cover their mouths with both hands and the *kittens* start saying, *"Meow, meow, meow"*. When the *Mother Cat* returns, she should listen carefully to find all of her *kittens*. When she has found them all, another child should be chosen *Mother Cat* and the game can continue.

CREATIVE THINKING At art have the children collage silhouettes of their pet or that of a friend. Have them bring the *pets* to circle time. Talk about how pets like to play with people in their family. Ask the children, *"How does your pet (or the pet of a friend) let you know when s/he wants to play?"* As the children answer, have them hold up their picture and name the kind of pet that they are talking about.

EXTENSION:
Ask additional questions such as, *"How does your pet let you know when he's hungry, wants to go outside, is tired, is angry, wants to be petted, wants a snack?"* and so on.

LANGUAGE GAMES

LOOK CAREFULLY Get large pictures of different pets. Cover up one part of each pet, such as a leg of the cat, the tail of the dog, fins of the goldfish and so on. Hold the pictures up one at a time and have the children tell you what part of the pet is hiding.

REMEMBER Say a series of three pets. Have the children repeat the series. Do this several times until you know they can remember those three. Increase the number of pets in the series. Continue challenging their memory, being careful not to exceed their abilities.

ACTIVE GAMES

COPY CATS Have one child be the 'cat' and clap a rhythm for the group. The other children listen and then be the 'Copy Cats'. They clap the same rhythm as the 'cat' did. Another child now becomes the 'cat' and creates a rhythm for the 'Copy Cats' to imitate.

ANIMAL TREATS Pets love treats. Before circle time hide granola cookies in the room. Have the children pretend to be a household pet and 'sniff' around to find the treats. When a child finds a cookie, have him/her return to the circle, do a 'trick' and then eat the cookie.

A
N
I
M
A
L
S

ACTIVE GAMES

OBEDIENCE TRAINING

Many household pets, especially dogs, go to Obedience School. Through obedience training, dogs learn many commands. Some are:

- *COME!*
- *HEEL!*
- *STAY!*
- *SIT!*
- *LAY DOWN!*

Have the children pretend to be dogs and you be the master. Give the commands to the children. Once the children understand the commands, have them pair off. One child can pretend to be the '*dog*' and the other can be the '*master*'. The '*master*' gives the commands to the child who is pretending to be the '*dog*'. Switch roles.

BOOKS

HELEN GRIFFITH — *MINE WILL, SAID JOHN*
EZRA JACK KEATS — *PET SHOW*
LIESEL SKORPEN — *ALL THE LASSIES*
RUTH TENSEN — *COME TO THE PET SHOP*

ZOO ANIMALS

FOR OPENERS

HAVE A VARIETY OF ZOO ANIMALS MADE OUT OF FELT. TAKE AN IMAGINARY WALK AROUND THE ZOO.

"IT WAS A BRIGHT, COOL MORNING AND OUR FAMILY DECIDED TO GO TO THE ZOO. WE QUICKLY PACKED A PICNIC LUNCH AND WERE OFF FOR THE DAY. WE ARRIVED AT THE GATE JUST AS THE ZOO WAS OPENING. AS WE WALKED IN, THERE WERE SEVERAL BLACK AND WHITE STRIPED ANIMALS RUNNING AROUND IN A FIELD BEHIND A FENCE. WHAT WERE THE FIRST ANIMALS WE SAW? (LET THE CHILDREN ANSWER AND THEN PUT THE PICTURE OF THAT ANIMAL ON THE FELT BOARD. THIS IS THE FORMAT FOR THE REST OF THE STORY.) OUR FAMILY CONTINUED WALKING ALONG THE PATH. SOON WE CAME TO AN ANIMAL THAT HAD A LONG GRAY TRUNK AND A HUGE BODY. (ANSWER, ELEPHANT.) WE STOOD WATCHING THE ELEPHANT FOR AWHILE. WE WOULD HAVE LIKED TO THROW HIM PEANUTS, BUT THERE WAS A SIGN THAT SAID, 'DO NOT FEED THE ELEPHANTS'. WE PROCEEDED ALONG WATCHING MANY OF THE ANIMALS ROMPING BEHIND THE DIFFERENT FENCES. AFTER AWHILE WE CAME TO ONE OF MY VERY FAVORITE ANIMALS. THIS ANIMAL HAD A LONG NECK, WAS YELLOW, AND WAS COVERED WITH BROWN SPOTS. (ANSWER, GIRAFFE.) WE STOOD THERE FOR AWHILE WATCHING THE GIRAFFE EAT LEAVES FROM THE TOP OF A TALL TREE. DAD SAID, 'LET'S BE ON OUR WAY. THERE ARE LOTS MORE ANIMALS TO ENJOY.' HE WAS RIGHT. THE VERY NEXT ONES WE SAW MADE US LAUGH ALL THE WHILE WE WATCHED THEM. THESE ANIMALS PLAYED ON TRAPEZES, LIKED TO SWING FROM BRANCHES, TIRES, AND ROPES. THEY WERE? (ANSWER, MONKEYS.) AS WITH MANY OF THE OTHER ANIMALS WE COULD HAVE ENJOYED THE MONKEYS ALL DAY, HOWEVER, IT WAS GETTING CLOSE TO LUNCHTIME. WE SAT ON THE PICNIC BENCH AND ATE. AS WE ENJOYED OUR SANDWICHES, A BEAUTIFUL BIRD WALKED BY AND FANNED HIS TAIL AT ME. IT HAD SO MANY COLORS IN IT. (ANSWER, PEACOCK.) LUNCH WAS OVER AND WE HAD ALL AFTERNOON TO WALK AROUND." CONTINUE THE STORY USING ZOO ANIMALS THAT YOUR CHILDREN WOULD IDENTIFY. AFTER TALKING ABOUT THREE OR FOUR MORE ANIMALS SAY, "THE SUN WAS SETTING AND WE WERE ALL VERY TIRED. WE AGREED THAT IT WAS ABOUT TIME TO GO HOME. WE STOPPED TO HAVE A DRINK AND THEN WENT TO THE CAR. THE NEXT THING I REMEMBER WAS THAT MOM AND DAD WERE CARRYING US INTO THE HOUSE."

ANIMALS

FINGERPLAYS

ONE, ONE, THE ZOO IS FUN

One, one, the zoo is fun.
Two, two, see a kangaroo.
Three, three, see a chimpanzee.
Four, four, hear the lions roar.
Five, five, see the seals dive.
Six, six, the monkey does tricks.
Seven, seven, elephants eleven.
Eight, eight, a tiger and his mate.
Nine, nine, birds in a line.
Ten, ten, I will come again.

BEARS EVERYWHERE

Bears, bears, bears everywhere!
Bears climbing stairs.
Bears sitting on chairs.
Bears collecting fares.
Bears giving stares.
Bears washing hairs.
Bears, bears, bears, everywhere!

THE YELLOW GIRAFFE

The yellow giraffe is tall as can be.
His lunch is a bunch of leaves off of a tree.
He has a long neck and his legs are long too.
He runs faster than his friends at the zoo.

FIVE LITTLE ELEPHANTS

Five little elephants
Rowing toward the shore,
One fell in.
And then there were four.

Four little elephants
Climbing up a tree,
One slid down.
Then there were three.

Three little elephants
Living in the zoo,
One walked off.
Then there were two.

Two little elephants
Playing in the sun,
One fell asleep.
Then there was one.

One little elephant
Isn't any fun.
Abra-ca-da-bra!
Then there were none!

RECIPES

Having a snack? Eat with the zoo
animals.

Bear — Apples and Vegetables
Elephant — Bread and vegetables
Giant panda — Carrots and apples
Giraffe — Legumes such as beans,
　　　　　apricots
Lion — Meat

FIELD TRIPS

● Enjoy a day at the local zoo. Try to arrive when it opens. It is less crowded and the children are not tired. Though it is fun to see all of the animals, concentrate on the ones that the children will recognize. As you observe each of the animals note what they are doing, how they move, and what they like to eat. If there is a 'children's zoo' within the main zoo, take time to visit that section also. Let the children see and pet the newborn animals. Do the young animals look like their parents?

LANGUAGE GAMES

FELT BOARD FUN ● Bears can be categorized by color, the brown bear, black bear and white bear. Using felt, make one adult and one baby bear out of each color. Put the adult bears on the felt board. Talk about them. Now put the three matching baby bears on the felt board. Have a child come up and match one of the baby bears with the parent. Let other children continue the matching game.

EXTENSION:
● Count all of the bears. Then count the pairs of bears. Talk about the meaning of the word 'pair'. Count the individual bears and the pairs again.

● Put the animals that you made for the OPENER WALK on the felt board. Ask the children, "Which one of these animals is the giraffe?" Have one child come up and point to it. Then ask, "How do you know that this animal is the giraffe?" Discuss the characteristics of the giraffe. Continue with the remaining animals.

● Using all of the felt animals, play WHAT'S MISSING. Put the animals on the board. Name them. Have the children cover their eyes and then take one of the animals away. Have the children uncover their eyes, look at all of the remaining animals and say which animal is missing. Put the animal back and play again.

LANGUAGE GAMES

LOOK CAREFULLY Get large pictures of lions, tigers, leopards, cheetahs and other wild cats. (The local library or zoo is a good source.) Tack all of the pictures on a board. Have the children look carefully at the pictures of the cats. *"How are they different? What characteristics are the same?"*

ROARING Go around the group and let each child be a *'big cat'* by roaring into the tape recorder. Play the tape back and see how many children recognize their own *'roar'*. See if any of the children can recognize the *'roars'* of their classmates.

TALK ABOUT Read the poem *"Elephant"*.
> *Right foot, left foot, see me go.*
> *I am gray and big and slow.*
> *I come walking down the street,*
> *With my trunk and four big feet.*

Once you have read the poem, ask the children, *"Who knows what zoo animal the poem is talking about? Who has seen a real elephant? What did it look like? Was it eating or drinking or doing something else?"* If the elephant was eating or drinking, let the child try to remember what was being eaten or drunk. *"How did the elephant get the food or drink to his mouth?"*

EXTENSION:
Read the poem again and let the children walk around the room pretending to be elephants. Let the children pretend to be elephants who are eating and drinking.

ACTIVE GAMES

BEAN BAG TOSS — Get a large box from the grocery store and four pieces of poster board. On each piece of poster board draw a large picture of a different zoo animal. With a marker, draw a ring around each animal's mouth. Staple one picture to each side of the box and put it in the middle of the circle.

Have four children with bean bags stand around the box. First have each child name the animal s/he is standing in front of. The rest of the children say "One, two three, toss!!" When they say "Toss!!", the four children throw their beanbags at the animals' mouths. Continue playing with other children naming the animals and tossing the bean bags.

BROWN BEAR — Enjoy this chant with the children. Let all of the children pretend to be bears doing these tricks as they chant.

> Brown bear, brown bear
>   Turn around.
> Brown bear, brown bear,
>   Touch the ground.
> Brown bear, brown bear,
>   Walk along.
> Brown bear, brown bear,
>   Sing a song.

(After you say the last line, have a child pick a song to sing. Everyone sing it. Say the *Brown Bear* poem again and have another child pick a song to sing. Do several more times.)

ANIMALS

BOOKS

EVE RICE — *SAM WHO NEVER FORGETS*
FEODOR ROJANKOWSKY — *ANIMALS IN THE ZOO*

WOODS ANIMALS

FOR OPENERS

FIND TWO PICTURES OF AS MANY WOODS ANIMALS AS YOU CAN — DEER, SQUIRREL, MOUSE, SKUNK, RABBIT, BIRD, ETC. MAKE INDIVIDUAL CARDS WITH ONE SET OF PICTURES AND A SPINNER BOARD WITH THE OTHER SET. DIVIDE A PIECE OF POSTERBOARD INTO AS MANY SECTIONS AS YOU HAVE ANIMALS. GLUE ONE PICTURE IN EACH SECTION. USE A BRAD TO SECURE THE SPINNER.

AT CIRCLE TIME, PASS THE CARDS OUT TO THE CHILDREN. HAVE A CHILD COME AND FLICK THE SPINNER. WHEN IT STOPS, HAVE THE GROUP CALL OUT THE NAME OF THE ANIMAL IT INDICATES. THE CHILD HOLDING THE PICTURE CARD OF THAT ANIMAL SHOULD PUT HIS / HER PICTURE IN THE MIDDLE OF THE CIRCLE AND SPIN THE POINTER. WHEN ALL OF THE CARDS ARE IN THE MIDDLE SAY, "RAMONA, GET THE PICTURE OF THE SKUNK." CONTINUE IN THIS MANNER UNTIL ALL OF THE CHILDREN HAVE A NEW PICTURE. PLAY THE SPINNER GAME AGAIN.

FINGERPLAYS

BUNNY

Here's a bunny,
With ears so funny.
Here is his hole in the ground.
He hears a noise and pricks up his ears.
He jumps into his home underground.

GRAY SQUIRREL

Gray squirrel, gray squirrel,
Swish your bushy tail.
Gray squirrel, gray squirrel,
Swish your bushy tail.
Wrinkle up your little nose.
Hold a nut between your toes.
Gray squirrel, gray squirrel,
Swish your bushy tail.

IF I WERE A BIRD

If I were a bird, I'd sing a song,
And fly about the whole day long.
And when the night comes, go to rest,
Up in my cozy little nest.

HOUSES

Here is a nest for a robin.
Here is a hive for a bee.
Here is a hole for a bunny.
And here is a house for ME!

BUMBLE BEE

Bright colored bumble bee
Looking for your honey,
Flap your wings and fly away
While it still is sunny.

RECIPES

Enjoy snacks that the woods animals also like.

Deer — Nuts and fruits
Rabbit — Greens and carrots
Skunk — Berries and fruit
Squirrel — Nuts and corn
Raccoon — Nuts, seeds, fruit, and corn

FIELD TRIPS

● Many woods animals can be observed in city parks, close by fields, and back yards. Go to any of these places. Sit very quietly and watch for the animals. See if you can see squirrels, birds, rabbits, and other forms of local wildlife. If you have a field or open area near your classroom, enjoy feeding the animals by hanging a bird feeder, putting out tubs of bread, anchoring bags of suet, etc. Remember, once you begin to feed the animals, they will depend on your food. Please do not stop until you are sure they can find another source of food.

LANGUAGE GAMES

LOOK CAREFULLY Get large, detailed pictures of different woods animals. (Ranger Rick and Geographic World are good sources.) Glue them to poster board. Hold one picture up at a time. First have the children name the animal and then 'call out' as many words as they can to describe the picture.

EXTENSION:
Tack four or five of the pictures to a piece of styrofoam or other type of board. Have the children cover their eyes. Take one animal away. Have the children uncover their eyes and 'whisper' the name of the animal you took away. After they have guessed, hold up the animal to see if they were right. Mix up the pictures and play again.

ANIMAL TALK   Talk about the sounds that different woods animals make. Let the children pretend that they are birds, squirrels, mice, raccoons, and other animals. Using animal noises, have the children talk to a partner in happy, angry, sad, and sleepy voices.

ANIMALS

LANGUAGE GAMES

APPLAUDE THE ANIMALS
Say a long series of words, some of which are woods animals and some of which are not —*rabbit, tree, pencil, squirrel, mouse, table,* and so on. Whenever the children hear you say a name of a woods animal, they should clap. When the word is not a woods animal, they should be quiet.

ANIMAL HUNT
Take a pretend walk looking for different woods animals. Have the children quietly tap their knees as if they were *'walking'*. While they are *'walking'*, have them look for animals. Have the children take turns calling out what pretend animals they see. When a child says an animal name, you should say, *"Beth, sees a nest of birds (or whatever the animal). Beth, clap the number of birds that you see."* Beth then claps the number of birds that she imagines she sees. The other children should count as Beth claps. After she has finished, all of the other children should say, *"Beth sees 4 birds."*

ACTIVE GAMES

SQUIRREL SCAMPER
Let the children pretend that they are squirrels getting ready for winter. Just before circle time, hide shelled peanuts around the room. Let the children scamper around and look for the nuts. When they find one, have them put it on a tray in the circle time area. Soon all of the nuts will have been piled on the tray. Enjoy eating them for a snack.

ACTIVE GAMES

MOVING Talk about how the different woods animals move.
- BIRDS FLY
- RABBITS HOP
- SQUIRRELS SCAMPER
- SNAKES CRAWL ON THEIR STOMACHS

Let the children each pick an animal s/he would like to be. Then move around the circle pretending to be that animal.

EXTENSION:
Have a 'Parade of Animals'. Have everyone choose the animal s/he would like to be. When everyone is ready, the parade can begin. Have the parade route go around the school or around the neighboorhood. If apropros, let the children make the noise of the animal s/he is pretending to be.

WISE OLD OWL Woods animals often move very quietly. Have one child stand in the center of the circle and be a 'wise old owl.' Have the 'owl' close his/her eyes, point randomly at a child and say the name of another woods animal. That child should move as quietly as s/he can toward the 'owl'. If the 'owl' hears the 'animal' moving s/he says, "I hear a noisy _____." and the child must go back. If not the 'animal' taps the 'owl'. The first 'owl' goes into the circle and the second child becomes the 'wise old owl'.

ANIMALS

BOOKS

RUTH KRAUSS — *THE HAPPY DAY*
GARTH WILLIAMS — *THE RABBITS WEDDING*

WATER ANIMALS

FOR OPENERS

NAME DIFFERENT CREATURES, SOME OF WHICH LIVE IN THE WATER AND SOME OF WHICH DO NOT. HAVE THE CHILDREN PRETEND TO SWIM IF THE CREATURE IS A WATER ANIMAL OR SHAKE THEIR HEADS "NO" IF IT IS NOT. HERE IS A LIST FOR STARTERS: TURTLE, SHARK, LION, MONKEY, ALLIGATOR, FISH, SEAL, BEAVER, ELEPHANT.

FINGERPLAYS

THE FISH
I hold my fingers like a fish,
And wave them as I go!
See them swimming with a swish,
So swiftly to and fro.

THIS IS MY TURTLE
This is my turtle.
He lives in a shell.
He likes his home so very well.
His head pokes out when he wants some food
And he pulls it in when sleep is his mood.

THREE FROGS
Three little frogs
Asleep in the sun.
We'll wake them up
And then we'll run.

MR. BULLFROG
Here's Mr. Bullfrog
Sitting on a rock.
Along comes a little girl (boy).
Mr. Bullfrog jumps, KERPLOP!!

FIELD TRIPS

● Many forest preserves, nature centers, and parks have rivers, streams, and/or lakes in them. Contact the ranger and schedule a trip to observe the water and the creatures who live in it. While there, see if you can find any of the animals' homes. Have the ranger tell the children what foods the animals eat.

LANGUAGE GAMES

GONE FISHING — Ask the children if any of them have ever gone fishing. Have them tell about their experience. *"Who has ever caught a fish? How? What did you do with the fish?"*

MEMORY — Give each child a picture of a water animal. Have the children look carefully at their picture. Go around the circle naming each type of animal. Then have the children sit on their picture. Now that all of the pictures are hidden, say, *"I'm looking for the picture of the whale. Whoever has it, stand up.* (That child stands.) *I'm looking for a picture of an angel fish. Whoever has it, hop up and down."* (That child hops.) Continue with all of the water animals.
VARIATION:
Instead of naming the water animal that you are looking for, describe it. *"I'm looking for a picture of a very large grey animal. The animal breathes air through a blow hole."* The child with the picture of the whale says, *"I have the whale."*

FELT BOARD FUN — Make a variety of water animals out of felt or back your pictures with felt. Using these and the felt animals that you made for the zoo and farm, play WHICH ONE DOESN'T BELONG? Have the children cover their eyes. Put three water animals and one from another category on the felt board. Have the children uncover their eyes and call out the name of the animal which does not belong. Also tell where that animal lives. Play frequently.
VARIATION:
Put several animals on the felt board which do not belong. Have the children find all of them.

LANGUAGE GAMES

CREATIVE THINKING

Ask the children questions such as,
  "If you had a whale for a pet, where would he live?"
  "If you were a porpoise, what would be your favorite trick?"
  (Let the children show their tricks.)
  "If you were a little fish and a giant fish was going to eat you, what would you do?"
  "What do you think the water animals do for fun?"

LISTEN AND THINK

Make different water animals during art. Bring them to circle time. Say statements about water animals, some of which are true and others which are false. When you say a true statement, have the children pretend that they are the water animal which they made in art swimming through the water. When the statement is false, the children should sit quietly.
  "Water animals live in water."
  "Some water animals breathe air."
  "Water animals are all colors."
  "Some water animals climb trees."
  "Some people like to catch water animals."
  "Water animals feed on each other."

ACTIVE GAMES

GO FISHING

Before circle time make a variety of animals who live in the water, such as whales, starfish, trout, jelly fish, sharks, and others that the children in your locale will be able to identify. Put a paper clip on each of the water animals. Make each child a 'fishing pole' by attaching a magnet to the end of a string which has been fastened to a stick such as a dowel rod.

Put the water animals in the middle of the circle. Let the children 'fish'. When a child has caught one, s/he should sit down. After everyone has an animal, go around the circle and identify each one.

FOLLOW THE FISH

Many fish swim in 'schools'. Talk about all of the movements that they make. Then have the children pretend that they are swimming in a 'school' by following a 'leader fish'. Have them swim, dive, eat, play, jump, rest, etc. as a 'school of fish' would.

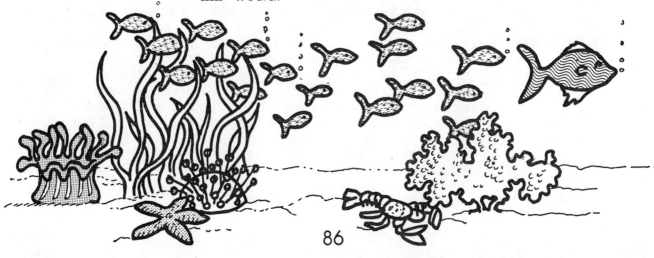

ACTIVE GAMES

PASS THE
SHARK

Make a shark and other water animals out of construction
paper or use plastic models. Have a 'pond' in the middle of
the circle time area marked off with a rope.

Bring all of the animals to circle time. Hold them up one
at a time and have the children call out the name of the
animal. Give each animal, except the shark, to a child to
put in the 'pond' Begin passing the shark around the circle.
As the children are passing the shark, have them chant:

Pass, pass, pass the shark.
Pass it very fast.
Pass, pass, pass, pass.
Let's see who is last!

The child holding the shark at the end of the chant, puts it
into the 'pond' and catches another animal. Chant again
using the name of the new animal. Continue.

ANIMALS

BOOKS

LEO LIONNI — *SWIMMY*
HELEN PALMER — *A FISH OUT OF WATER*

VEGETABLES

FOR OPENERS

MAKE A VARIETY OF VEGETABLES OUT OF COLORED FELT OR FIND PICTURES OF VEGETABLES AND BACK THEM WITH FELT.

GIVE ONE VEGETABLE TO EACH CHILD. HAVE EACH CHILD NAME THE VEGETABLE HE / SHE IS HOLDING. PRETEND THE FELT BOARD IS THE VEGETABLE BASKET, HAVE ONE CHILD PUT HIS / HER VEGETABLE IN THE BASKET. THEN GIVE ANOTHER CHILD A DIRECTION LIKE, "SASHA, PUT YOUR CARROT **UNDER** THE TOMATO." GIVE DIRECTIONS TO EACH CHILD USING A VARIETY OF POSITION WORDS, SUCH AS OVER, IN FRONT OF, NEXT TO, IN BACK OF, ON TOP OF, BEHIND, AND SO ON. SOON ALL OF THE VEGETABLES WILL BE IN THE VEGETABLE BASKET.

EXTENSION: WHEN THE VEGETABLES ARE IN THE BASKET ASK QUESTIONS LIKE:
"WHAT VEGETABLES ARE NEXT TO THE POTATO?"
"WHICH VEGETABLES ARE NEAR THE LETTUCE?"
"NAME ALL THE VEGETABLES UNDER THE CORN."

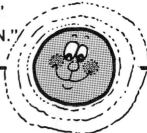

FINGERPLAYS

VEGETABLE GARDEN

I have a special piece of land
Just outside my door.
It's going to be a garden,
With vegetables galore.

First I planted carrots,
Which grow below the ground,
With bushy green tops above,
They easily can be found.

Next I put tomato plants
Which grow so very wide.
I'll stake them up to spread them out
So none of them will hide.

Also there are cucumbers.
These I planted in a mound,
So they can grow every which way
Right along the ground.

Finally there are potatoes,
These are funny too.
They grow on roots below the soil
To dig when the summer's through.

If you didn't plant a garden,
I certainly wonder why.
If you don't grow your own vegetables,
Then each one you must buy.
                              Dick Wilmes

RECIPES

STONE SOUP

Read the book STONE SOUP by Marcia Brown, then make the soup with the children.

YOU'LL NEED

1 large gray stone, scrubbed
6 cups of water
3 large carrots
2 onions
6 beef bouillion cubes
4 stalks of celery
3 large potatoes
4 tomatoes
1 cup chopped cabbage
1 t. salt
Pepper to taste

TO MAKE: Scrub the stone. Scrub and chop all of the vegetables. Cook all of the ingredients for about an hour.

FIELD TRIPS

• Make an appointment to visit the produce section of the grocery store nearest the center. If possible pick one within walking distance. Have the produce attendant show the children where the vegetables are received and stored, how they are processed, weighed, priced, and put on shelves for the customers to buy.

While at the produce section buy the vegetables you are going to have for lunch. Let the children help you pick them out. When you return to the center, you can fix the vegetables or give them to the cook.

F
O
O
D
S

NECTARINES 53¢ lb. SEEDLESS GRAPES 98¢ lb. GRAPEFRUIT 25¢ each PINEAPPLE $1.98 each

LANGUAGE GAMES

CATEGORIZING VEGETABLES

Have a tray of ten or more different vegetables. Hold each vegetable up for everyone to see. Name it and then pass it around for each child to hold and examine. When all of the vegetables have been passed around, put them in one group in front of you. Point to each vegetable. As you touch it, have the children call out its name.

Once the children have had the opportunity to name and examine the vegetables, play a categorizing game. Say to the children, *"Let's figure out how we can separate this pile of vegetables into two piles. One way we could do it would be by texture. The ones with smooth sides could go in one pile and the ones with bumpy sides in another. Let's try it."* Have a child come up, get a vegetable, feel it and say whether it should be in the *smooth* or *bumpy* pile. Put it there. Continue until all of the vegetables have been sorted. Then put all of the vegetables back into one pile and ask, *"Who can think of another way to sort these vegetables?"* Use the children's ideas (or your own) to categorize several more times.

WHICH ONE DOESN'T BELONG

Say a series of four words, three of which are vegetables and one which is not a vegetable. For example, *"Carrot, broccoli, dog, onion."* The children should listen to all of the words. After you have said the four words, have the children call out the word that was not a vegetable.
VARIATION:
Say the series of vegetables and non-vegetables. Have a child repeat all of the vegetables.

LISTEN CAREFULLY

Cut small pieces of various raw vegetables, such as carrots, lettuce, cauliflower, broccoli, tomatoes, mushrooms, cucumbers, etc. Pass each child a piece of the same vegetable. Name the vegetable and then eat it. While chewing the vegetable, have the children decide if it is crunchy or quiet.

ACTIVE GAMES

PETER RABBIT   Read the story of Peter sneaking around Mr. McGregor's vegetable garden. After you have read it, have the children hold hands to form a circle. Pretend the inside of the circle is the vegetable garden. Have one child in the middle pretending to be Peter and another child outside the circle, pretending to be Mr. McGregor. Peter is trying to escape from the garden before Mr. McGregor catches him. The children try to help Peter escape by lifting their arms up and down to let Peter out, but not let Mr. McGregor in.

SINGING   Sing this song to the tune of *"HERE WE GO 'ROUND THE MULBERRY BUSH."*

> *First the farmer plows the ground,*
> *Plows the ground, plows the ground.*
> *First the farmer plows the ground,*
> *Then he plants the seeds.*
>
> *This is the way he plants the seeds,*
> *So that they will grow.*
>
> *The rain and sun will help them grow,*
> *Right up through the ground.*
>
> *Now the farmer picks the corn,*
> *And we have food to eat.*

FOODS

BOOKS

TANA HOBAN — *WHERE IS IT?*
VIRGINIA POULET — *BLUE BUG'S VEGETABLE GARDEN*

PUMPKINS

FOR OPENERS

BUY TWO BAKING PUMPKINS. WASH THE PUMPKINS WITH THE CHILDREN. PUT ONE OF THEM IN A BAKING PAN AND BAKE AT 325 DEGREES FOR ABOUT AN HOUR OR UNTIL SOFT. LET IT COOL.

BRING THE UNCOOKED AND COOKED PUMPKINS TO CIRCLE TIME. LET THE CHILDREN FIRST EXAMINE THE OUTSIDE OF THE PUMPKINS. PASS THEM AROUND. SMELL THEM AND FEEL THEM. TALK ABOUT THE DIFFERENCES. THEN CUT THE COOKED ONE OPEN. PASS IT AROUND FOR THE CHILDREN TO SEE. CUT THE UNCOOKED ONE OPEN. PASS IT AROUND ALSO. (PUT IT IN THE DISCOVERY AREA AFTER CIRCLE TIME.) CUT THE COOKED PUMPKIN INTO SMALLER PIECES. GIVE EACH CHILD A PIECE ALONG WITH A CUP OR PLASTIC CONTAINER. LET EACH CHILD TAKE THE SEEDS OUT OF HIS / HER PIECE AND PUT THEM IN THE CUP. WHEN THE PUMPKIN IS ALL CLEANED, PASS OUT SPOONS AND LET THE CHILDREN EAT THEIR PIECE OF PUMPKIN. TALK ABOUT THE TASTE AS THEY EAT.

FINGERPLAYS

TOMMY'S PUMPKINS
It was the biggest pumpkin
That I had ever seen.
It grew in Tommy's garden
Until the night of Halloween.

(Ask the children what might have happened to Tommy's pumpkin.)

PUMPKIN PIE
My father bought a pumpkin
And much to my surprise,
We didn't carve a funny face
We made two pumpkin pies.
Dick Wilmes

RECIPES

PUMPKIN BREAD
YOU'LL NEED

½ cup vegetable oil
¾ cup honey
1 t. molasses
2 cups pumpkin
2 cups whole wheat flour
2 t. baking soda
1 t. cloves
1 t. cinnamon
½ t. salt
1 cup chopped nuts

TO MAKE: Cream the shortening and honey together. Beat the eggs well. Mash the pumpkin. Chop the nuts. Mix all of these ingredients together with the dry ingredients. Grease one 5" by 9" loaf pan. Pour the batter into the pan. Bake at 350 degrees for about 45 to 60 minutes. Test with a toothpick. Loosen the sides and cool on a wire rack.
from COME AND GET IT
by Kathleen Baxter

FIELD TRIPS

● Visit a pumpkin farm. As the children are walking around the field have them notice how the pumpkins grow, the different colors of pumpkins, their shapes, and textures. Let the children choose a pumpkin to bring home. Have them really search around the field before they pick the one they want. When they finally decide, be certain that it is one they can carry themselves.

LANGUAGE GAMES

PUMPKIN BOOK   When you return from the pumpkin farm, have each child make a picture of the trip for your PUMPKIN BOOK. Then have him/her dictate a sentence or two about the trip. When the book is completed, bring it to circle time. Read it to the children. As you read the page each child created, have that child stand up. If s/he would like to say something else about the trip, let him/her do so.

LANGUAGE GAMES

HOW MANY PUMPKINS?

Using pumpkin stickers, make a variety of flash cards with a different number of pumpkins on each one. Then make number cards with only the numbers on them.

At circle time give each child a card with pumpkins on it. Spread the number cards out on the floor in the middle of the circle. Have a child stand up, count the pumpkins on his/her card aloud, and then find the number card in the center of the circle that matches the amount of pumpkins on the card. Continue by matching the cards of all of the children.

PUMPKIN MATCH

Before circle time make a *'flip book'* of different sizes and shapes of pumpkins. First cut seven or eight pages out of orange poster board. On every page, except the one to be used for the back cover, draw a different size or shape pumpkin. (Use bold lines.) Next cut each pumpkin in half and punch matching holes in each one, plus holes on the top and bottom of the back. Put a metal ring (or tie with yarn) through the top pictures and another one through the bottom pictures.

Bring the book to circle time. Begin flipping the bottom set of pictures until you get to the one that matches the top half. Discuss the shape and size. *"Is this the shape that you use at Halloween to carve a jack-o-lantern? Would this pumpkin make a happy jack-o-lantern or a scary one?"*

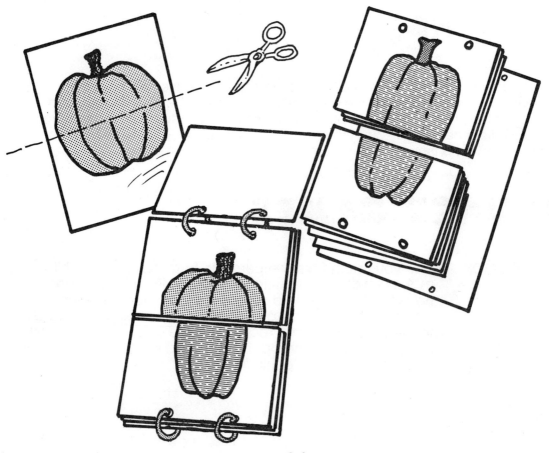

ACTIVE GAMES

PASS THE PUMPKIN   Get a small pumpkin. Have the children sit in a circle. Play some music. As the music plays, have the children pass the pumpkin around the circle. When the music stops, the child holding the pumpkin gets a pumpkin sticker to wear on his/her hand.

Kevin's   Amy's   Erica's

TAPE THE STEM ON THE PUMPKIN   At art, have the children make pumpkins without stems. (You make an adequate number of stems for the game.) Have the children bring their pumpkins to circle time. As they arrive, tack each pumpkin low on a bulletin board near the circle area. Give each child a stem with a piece of tape looped on the back of it. Have each child cover his/her eyes and walk toward the pumpkins with the stem in his/her hand. Guide the child's hand near his/her pumpkin. Let him/her feel around the pumpkin and then stick the stem where s/he wants. Let the child uncover his/her eyes and see where the stem is.

As each child is putting the stem on his/her pumpkin, the other children can chant:

Pumpkin, pumpkin without a stem,
Laying in the pumpkin patch,
Here comes Billy to look for you
With a stem of brown to match.

BOOKS

DAHLOV IPCAR — *BRING IN THE PUMPKINS*
EDNA MILLER — *MOUSEKIN'S GOLDEN HOUSE*

FRUITS

FOR OPENERS

PLAY "FRUIT MATCH". FIND PICTURES OF BETWEEN TWELVE AND SIXTEEN DIFFERENT FRUITS. DIVIDE A LARGE PIECE OF POSTERBOARD INTO AN EQUAL NUMBER OF SECTIONS. GLUE ONE FRUIT INTO EACH SECTION. BUY SOME OF EACH TYPE OF FRUIT FOR WHICH YOU HAVE A PICTURE. PUT ALL OF THE FRUITS INTO A BAG.

HOLD UP THE BOARD. POINT TO EACH PICTURE AND HAVE THE CHILDREN CALL OUT THE NAMES OF THE FRUITS THEY RECOGNIZE. PUT THE BOARD IN THE MIDDLE OF THE CIRCLE. TAKE A PIECE OF FRUIT OUT OF THE BAG. GIVE IT TO A CHILD. HAVE HIM / HER HOLD IT UP AND THE OTHERS CALL OUT ITS NAME. THEN HAVE THE CHILD MATCH IT TO THE PICTURE ON THE BOARD. CONTINUE IN THIS WAY UNTIL ALL OF THE REAL FRUITS HAVE BEEN IDENTIFIED AND MATCHED. ENJOY EATING SEVERAL OF THE FRUITS FOR A SNACK.

FINGERPLAYS

THE FRUIT STAND

A rainbow full of colors you will see,
When you visit the fruit stand today with me.
Cases full of oranges stacked so high,
Then bushels of red apples will catch your eye.

Yellow bananas, grapes that are green,
Pineapples, melons, and peaches between.
Berries in colors, red, black, and blue.
Cherries, pears, and tangerines too.

So come to the fruit stand,
Come have a treat
With the sweetness of candy
And better to eat!
                    Dick Wilmes

FIVE ORANGES

Five oranges growing on a tree,
Three for you and two for me.
Let us shake the tree just so,
And five oranges will fall below.

1, 2, 3, 4, 5.

RECIPES

FRUIT KABOBS
YOU'LL NEED
Rounded toothpicks
Melons
Bananas
Apples
And other fresh fruits
TO MAKE: Clean all of the fruits. Cut them into small pieces and put several on each toothpick.

ORANGE JUICE
YOU'LL NEED
Hand juicer
Juice oranges, about one orange per child
TO MAKE: Cut the oranges in half, take out the seeds, and let each child squeeze the orange halves according to the directions on the juicer.

LANGUAGE GAMES

FRUIT PIN-UP   Cut out pictures of a variety of fruits that are popular in your locale. As the children come to circle time, tape a picture on each of their backs. Tell everyone **not** to tell each other what the picture is.

When everyone has gathered, have one child stand up and turn around so that everyone can see his/her fruit. Have several of the other children give clues about his/her fruit, such as *"It has red skin and white insides."* Now let the child try to guess what fruit s/he is. When the child guesses correctly, have him/her pull the picture off and hold it. Continue by letting each child try to guess what type of fruit is taped on his/her back.

FRUIT SALAD   Pretend that you are going to make a fruit salad for lunch. The first child names a fruit s/he would like to have in the salad. The group says, *"In the salad is an apple."* The next child names another fruit. The group then repeats both fruits. Continue around the circle trying to remember all of the fruits in the salad.

LANGUAGE GAMES

FRUIT TASTE
Enjoy a FRUIT TASTE. Bring a tray of matching dried/fresh fruits to circle time — pineapple, grapes, apricots, coconuts, plums, apples, bananas, etc. Let everyone have the opportunity to taste each type of fresh and dried fruit. After tasting each one, talk about the tastes.

NAME THAT FRUIT
Have a bag filled with fresh fruit. Have a child come up, pull out a piece, and give it to another child. That child should name the fruit and then put it in a basket. Pass the bag of fruit to another child. S/he should take out a piece of fruit and name it. Continue until all of the fruit has been selected, identified, and put in the basket.

ACTIVE GAMES

MUSICAL FRUIT
Have one piece of fruit for each child. Have the children stand in a circle and put their piece of fruit on a small plate in front of them. Ask one child to give you his/her fruit. When the music begins, have the children begin walking around the circle. When the music stops, have the children stop in front of a piece of fruit. One child will not have a piece of fruit. This child gets to choose any piece of fruit from the circle and go to snack. Continue in this manner until only one child is left. The last child gets the original piece of fruit that was removed at the beginning of circle time.

SIMON SAYS
Simon gives a variety of commands in relationship to fruits:
Simon says, *"Peel a banana."*
"Pick apples from a tree."
"Crack a coconut."
"Squish the grapes."
"Eat the cherries, but be careful for the pits."
"Squeeze the oranges."

BOOKS

ERIC CARLE — *VERY HUNGRY CATERPILLER*
ROBERT MCCLOSKEY — *BLUEBERRIES FOR SAL*
RUTH ORBACH — *APPLE PIGS*

APPLES

FOR OPENERS

GIVE EACH CHILD AN APPLE. FIRST EXPLORE THE OUTSIDE OF THE APPLE. TALK ABOUT THE COLOR, SHAPE, TEXTURE, SMELL, AND SO ON. WHEN FINISHED, QUICKLY GO AROUND TO EACH CHILD AND CUT EACH APPLE IN HALF. PUT ONE HALF IN A BOWL AND LET THE CHILDREN KEEP THE OTHER HALF TO EXPLORE. NOW DISCUSS THE INSIDE OF THE APPLE.

> "WHAT COLORS DO YOU SEE NOW?"
> "ARE ANY OF THEM THE SAME AS THE OUTSIDE
>   OF THE APPLE?"
>
> "WHAT IS INSIDE THE APPLE?"
>
> "DOES THE INSIDE OF THE APPLE SMELL?"
> "LIKE WHAT?"

NOW ROLL OUT A LONG SHEET OF NEWSPRINT. PUT SEVERAL SHALLOW PANS OF RED TEMPERA PAINT ALONG THE PAPER. HAVE THE CHILDREN GET SMOCKS AND ENJOY 'APPLE PRINTING' A MURAL. WHEN IT IS DRY, HANG IT UP FOR EVERYONE TO ENJOY.

PASS THE CLEAN APPLE HALVES AROUND FOR A SNACK.

FINGERPLAYS

APPLE BUDS

Here are two apple buds growing on a tree,
Curled up very tightly, as buds should be.
Along came the sun one day shining from the sky,
And two little apple buds opened up their eye.

IF I WERE AN APPLE

If I were an apple and grew on a tree,
I think I'd drop down on a nice child like me.
I wouldn't stay there "hanging around"
I'd fall down very softly and hope to be found.

APPLES

Way up high in the apple tree,
Two little apples smiled at me,
I shook that tree as hard as I could,
Down came the apples,
Um, um, good!!

OUCH

Apple green, apple red,
An apple fell upon my head!
Dick Wilmes

APPLE TREE

Here is a tree with its leaves so green.
Here are the apples that hang in between.
When the wind blows, the apples will fall.
Here is a basket to gather them all.

FOODS

99

RECIPES

APPLE-DATE COOKIES

YOU'LL NEED

1 cup of dates
½ cup of water
1 cup of shredded raw apple
1¾ cup of applesauce
½ cup chopped walnuts
½ t. salt
1 t. vanilla
¼ cup chopped dates
3 cups rolled oats

TO MAKE: Combine the dates and water in a small pan. Heat, mash, and stir until smooth. Add the applesauce and beat until the mixture is smooth. Add the other ingredients. Mix well. Let stand about 10 minutes to absorb the moisture. Beat briskly. Drop the mixture from a teaspoon onto an ungreased cookie sheet. Bake at 375 degrees for 25 minutes or until nicely browned. Makes about 3 dozen cookies.
from A FAMILY AFFAIR: SNACKS by Aviva Croll

BAKED APPLES

YOU'LL NEED

1 apple for each person
Dash of cinnamon
½ t. butter
1 t. maple syrup
1 T. water
Extra delights such as raisins and walnuts

TO MAKE: Take the core out of each apple without cutting through the bottom. Fill each apple with butter, cinnamon, syrup, and raisins and walnuts if desired. Put the apples in a baking dish. Bake at 350 degrees for 45 minutes. Serve warm or cold.
from COME AND GET IT by Kathleen Baxter

FIELD TRIPS

● Visit an apple orchard which has facilities for picking your own apples. Have one of the workers show the children around the orchard. Explain the variety of apples, what the apples are primarily used for (eating, baking, canning, drying, etc.), and how the orchard workers take care of the trees so as to get the most apples from the tree.

Once the children have been shown around the orchard, let them have the opportunity to pick apples from the trees.

LANGUAGE GAMES

APPLE MURAL   Cut a huge apple shape out of newsprint or another type of big paper. At art, let the children do apple printing on the shape. Bring the giant apple to circle time. Have the children play a variety of games with the printed apple.
- Count all of the apple prints.
- Find the print that is the largest/smallest.
- Find the print that is the darkest/lightest.
- Do any of the shapes look different than the others? Which ones? Why?

FELT BOARD FUN   Make a tree with five or more apples hanging from it. Put them on the felt board and tell this number story. As you use a child's name, have him/her come and take an apple from the tree. *"There were five big, juicy red apples hanging on the apple tree in the orchard. Julie was running through the orchard on her way to visit a friend. As she passed the tree, she jumped up and picked one. Now there were four apples on the tree. Adam and Larry were also romping in that orchard. They had been playing tag and were very hungry. When they saw those apples they just had to each have one. They reached up and picked two more. Now there were only two left. Carrie was walking her dog through the orchard. She had not had a snack yet. Who do you think ate the next apple?* (Let the children guess.)*Before any more children came along a family of worms crawled out to that last apple and ate most of it up. When the wind came along, the core fell to the ground. Now there were no apples left on the apple tree in the orchard."*

FOLLOW MY DIRECTIONS   Bring several dozen apples to circle time. Have a child come up and take a designated number of apples and put them in a group someplace inside the circle. Have another child come up and take a different number of apples and put them someplace else in the circle. Continue until you have five or six piles of apples in the circle.

    Now give specific directions to each child. Vary these according to each child's ability. *"Brian, hop to the pile which has four apples in it. Take one apple for yourself and bring one to me."* or *"Jose, crawl to the pile which has six apples. Take one to Sasha."* Continue.

101

ACTIVE GAMES

RUN FOR THE
APPLE

The children should stand in a circle holding hands. One child walks around the outside of the circle holding an apple. As s/he passes two children, s/he taps their hands and says, *"Run for the apple!"* The children run around the circle in opposite directions. As soon as they have left, the first child puts the apple in the vacated space and stands beside it. The first child to get back to the apple and pick it up becomes *'It'* and the game goes on.

DAWN ZAVODSKY

SINGING

Sing to the tune of *"SKIP TO MY LOU"*.
> *Pick some apples off my tree,*
> *Pick some apples off my tree,*
> *Pick some apples off my tree,*
> *Pick them all for you and me.*
> DAWN ZAVODSKY

Sing to the tune of *"THE MUFFIN MAN"*.
> *Did you see my apple tree,*
> *My apple tree,*
> *My apple tree?*
> *Did you see my apple tree,*
> *Full of apples red?*
> DAWN ZAVODSKY

BOOKS

CLYDE BULLA — *A TREE IS A PLANT*
JULIAN SCHEER — *RAIN MAKES APPLESAUCE*

BREADS

FOR OPENERS

THROUGHOUT THE YEARS BREAD HAS BEEN ONE OF MEN AND WOMEN'S MAIN FOODS. THERE ARE MANY TYPES OF BREADS: YEAST, SOURDOUGH, SWEET, CORN-MEAL, AND BAKING POWDER TO NAME ONLY A FEW.

EACH DAY MAKE A DIFFERENT TYPE OF BREAD WITH YOUR CLASS. BECAUSE EACH BREAD TAKES MORE OR LESS TIME, BE SURE TO SCHEDULE YOUR BAKING AC-CORDINGLY. WHEN THE BREAD HAS BAKED AND COOLED, LET EVERYONE ENJOY A PIECE. AS THE DAYS GO ON, BE SURE TO COMPARE THE TASTES, SMELLS, PREPARATION AND SO ON.

RECIPES

GINGERBREAD

YOU'LL NEED

½ cup of butter
¾ cup of molasses
3 eggs
1 cup sour milk
2 cups whole wheat flour
¼ t. ginger
½ t. allspice
1 rounded t. cinnamon
1 t. salt
1 t. baking soda
¼ t. cloves

TO MAKE: Cream the butter and molasses together. Add the eggs and beat well. Measure all of the dry ingredients into a sifter. Add the dry and wet ingredients alternately. Mix well after each addition. Grease a 9" by 13" pan. Fill with the batter. Bake at 375 degrees for 30 minutes. Serve warm or cool.
from COME AND GET IT
by Kathleen Baxter

BISCUITS

YOU'LL NEED

1 cup whole wheat flour
1 cup unbleached flour
¾ cup shortening
2 T. baking powder
½ t. salt
⅔ cup buttermilk

TO MAKE: Mix all of the dry ingredients. Add the buttermilk. Drop a heaping T. of the dough onto a cookie sheet. Bake at 425 degrees for about 10-12 minutes. Makes 12 biscuits.
from COME AND GET IT
by Kathleen Baxter

F O O D S

RECIPES

BANANA NUT BREAD

YOU'LL NEED

¼ cup butter
½ cup honey
2 eggs
3 mashed bananas
2 cups of whole wheat flour
⅛ t. salt
1 t. baking soda
¾ cup chopped nuts
3 T. buttermilk

TO MAKE: Cream the butter and honey together. Beat the eggs well. Mash the fruit and chop the nuts. Mix all of these ingredients together. Stir in the dry ingredients. Grease a 5" by 9" loaf pan. Bake at 350 degrees for 40 to 60 minutes. Test with a toothpick. Cool on a wire rack and slice.
from COME AND GET IT
by Kathleen Baxter

CORN BREAD

YOU'LL NEED

2 eggs
4 T. honey
1 cup whole wheat flour
2 cups yellow corn meal
1 t. salt
1 rounded t. baking soda
2 cups buttermilk
2 T. vegetable oil

TO MAKE: Beat the eggs and honey together. Measure and sift the dry ingredients, mix alternately with the milk. After everything is mixed, add the oil. Grease a 9" by 13" pan. Bake at 425 degrees for 30 minutes. Serve with butter and honey.
from COME AND GET IT
by Kathleen Baxter

FIELD TRIPS

● Before visiting a local bakery, have several cooking experiences with the children in which they made bread from scratch. Let them mix the ingredients, knead the dough, watch it rise, and then bake it. When making one or two loaves of bread it is all done by hand. When visiting the bakery have the baker show the children how the different machines help him/her make many loaves of bread, rolls, and cakes.

LANGUAGE GAMES

WHO'S GOT THE BREAD?

Bring four or five different types of bread (keep in plastic bags) to circle time. Hold up each type and have the children call out what kind of bread it is.

Then have a child sit in the middle and cover his/her eyes. Give another child one type of bread and have him/her put it behind his/her back. All of the other children put their hands behind their backs too. The child with the bread says, *"The bagels are so good."* After that, the child in the middle uncovers his/her eyes and tries to guess who has the bagels. As s/he guesses, s/he says, *"Byran has the bagels."* That child says *"Yes"* or *"No"*. Continue until the child in the middle guesses who has the bagels. The child with the bagels goes in the middle and covers his/her eyes. The game is played as before with another type of bread.

EXTENSION:

If the breads have been kept in plastic bags, have them for snack.

LOOK CAREFULLY

Give each child a homestyle or family type magazine. Have each child look through the pages until they find a picture of some type of bread. When they find a picture, have them stand up, show the others the picture, and call on someone to name the type of bread pictured. Keep going through all of the pictures.

REMEMBER

Start with the child sitting next to you. Let him/her say a type of bread. Then everyone repeats, *"Margaret likes pita bread."* Go to the next child and let him/her say a bread s/he likes. Now go back to the first child, repeat that bread and the second one. Go to a third child and on around the circle in this manner.

ACTIVE GAMES

BREAD HOP

Get a window shade. Draw a hopscotch grid on it with a heavy black marker. Draw (or glue) a picture of a different type of bread in each square. (Loaf, bagel, muffin, biscuit, hot dog bun, hamburger bun, french bread, crescent, hard roll, sweet bread, etc.) Tape the window shade to the floor in the circle time area.

As the children sit around the window shade, have one child start at the beginning and hop to a certain type of bread as you direct, such as, *"Lin hop to the hot dog bun."* As Lin is hopping the others chant:

Lin is hopping, hopping, hopping. . .
(Keep saying *"hopping"* until the child gets to the hot dog bun. You can chant in rhythm to the speed which Lin hops.)
Hopping to the hot dog bun.

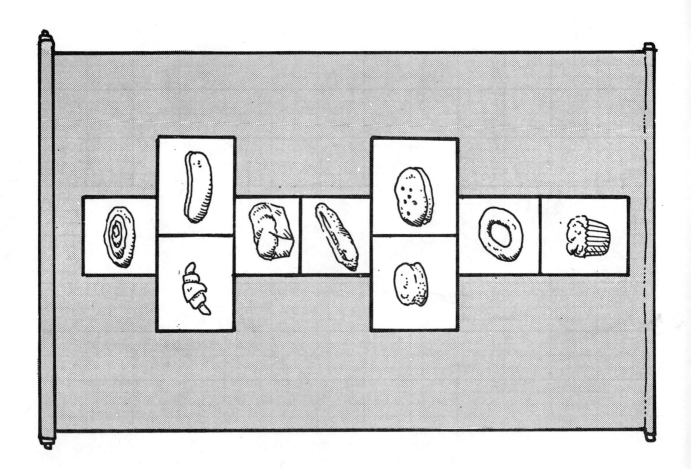

BOOKS

ELEANOR COERR — *MIXED-UP MYSTERY SMELL*
WENDE & HARRY DEVLIN — *CRANBERRY THANKSGIVING*

POPCORN

FOR OPENERS

POPCORN IS A FOOD THAT HAS BEEN ENJOYED FOR THOUSANDS OF YEARS. IT IS JUST ONE OF MANY VARIETIES OF CORN. (SEVERAL OTHER VARIETIES ARE SWEET CORN, INDIAN CORN, FIELD CORN, AND SO ON.)

HAVE A 'POPCORN HUNT' WITH THE CHILDREN. BEFORE THE CHILDREN COME TO SCHOOL, GET THE POPCORN POPPER ALL READY TO MAKE POPCORN. HIDE THE POPPER NEAR A PLUG. JUST BEFORE CIRCLE TIME PLUG IT IN.

BEGIN THE CIRCLE TIME AS YOU NORMALLY WOULD. SOON THE CHILDREN WILL BEGIN TO HEAR AND SMELL THE KERNELS POPPING. AS THEY GET MORE CURIOUS, TALK ABOUT WHAT IS HAPPENING. WHEN THEY THINK THEY KNOW WHERE IT IS, WALK OVER THERE AND SEE. WHEN THEY FIND IT, LET THE POPCORN FINISH POPPING. BRING IT TO THE CIRCLE TIME AREA AND ENJOY IT FOR A SNACK.

FINGERPLAYS

THE POPCORN KERNEL

I am a popcorn kernel,
On the electric range,
With oil to my ankles,
Waiting for the change.

Pop, pop, its started happening,
The noise has just begun.
Pop, pop, there it goes again.
It sounds like lots of fun.

Explosions to the left of me.
Explosions to the right.
I'm just about to blow my top,
I really think I might.
      BANG!!!!
        Dick Wilmes

EZ POPPER

Take a little oil.
Take a little seed.
Put them in a popper,
And heat is all you need.
        Dick Wilmes

RECIPES

CARAMEL CORN

YOU'LL NEED

4½ quarts of salted popcorn
½ cup butter
⅓ cup honey
1 cup brown sugar
1 t. vanilla
Peanuts (optional)

TO MAKE: Gently boil the butter, honey, and brown sugar together. (Do not let the mixture burn.) Remove from the heat and add vanilla. Pour over the popcorn and peanuts. Stir the mixture. Place the mixture on a cookie sheet and bake for about an hour at 250 degrees. (Stir it often to prevent burning.) Immediately put the mixture on wax paper. When cool break it apart and have for a snack.

CHOW MEIN POPCORN

YOU'LL NEED

1 cup of Chow Mein Noodles
¼ cup of butter
2 quarts popped popcorn
¼ t. salt

TO MAKE: In a small skillet melt ¼ cup of butter. Add the chow mein noodles and cook for 2 minutes, stirring several times. Pour over freshly popped popcorn. Salt to taste and toss well.
from A FAMILY AFFAIR: SNACKS by Aviva Croll

LANGUAGE GAMES

POPCORN
EXPLOSION

Place a large sheet on the floor in the circle time area. Have the children sit around the edge of it. Put a popcorn popper in the middle of the sheet. As you talk with the children about the process of making popcorn, pop some leaving the top of the popper off. As the popcorn starts to pop, several kernels will explode and fly out. As the activity proceeds, more and more kernels will come flying out of the popper. By popping corn in this way the children will better understand what happens as the kernels are popping inside the popper. (Be certain to take the necessary safety precautions.)

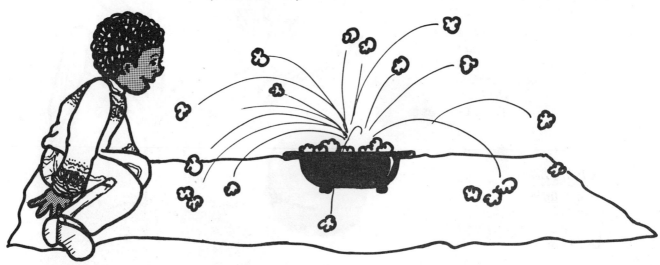

LANGUAGE GAMES

POPCORN BOOK Take a series of pictures of the children making Caramel Popcorn. When the pictures are developed, mount them onto sheets of construction paper, leaving space at the bottom for the children's words. Make the pages into a book showing popcorn being popped and the caramel being added. At circle time show the children and pictures and have them tell you what to write under each picture. When the book is completed, read it to the children. Then put it on the book shelf for everyone to enjoy even more.

MEMORY Once the children have had the experience of popping corn several times, talk about the steps to making it. *"Let's think about making popcorn. First we need to _____. After we've plugged in the popper, we add the _____ and _____. When the several kernels pop we know that the oil is hot enough to _____. All of the kernels make so much noise as they are popping. But soon the noise gets softer, softer, softer, and then no noise. That lets us know that _____. We put the popcorn in a bowl and add _____. Then the best part. We _____ it. Yum! Yum!*

ACTIVE GAMES

POPCORN TRAIL Go out to a park, field, or playground. Divide the class into two groups. Give each child in one group some popcorn kernels and have the children in the other group cover their eyes. With the teacher's help, the group with the kernels should leave a trail of popcorn between the starting place and a hideout. After the trail is made and the children have crouched down to hide, the second group of children should uncover their eyes and begin to follow the POP-CORN TRAIL. When they get to the end of the trail, the hiding group should jump up and say *"Boo!"* Go to another section of the playground and reverse the groups. Play the game again. (The birds and woods animals will eat the dropped kernels so that you need not worry about 'littering'.)

109

ACTIVE GAMES

PARACHUTE
PLAY

Enjoy using your parachute (sheet) as a 'popcorn popper'. Bring the parachute and ping pong balls to circle time. To begin, have the children sit around the parachute and give each child several balls. "*We are going to make some popcorn today and we need everyone's help. Our parachute is going to be the popper and these ping pong balls are the popcorn. First let's plug in the popper.* (Everyone pretend to plug in the popper.)*Pour in the oil* (Pour)*and a few kernels.* (You toss in several balls.)*When these kernels get hot enough they will pop. It won't take long.* (After several seconds wave the parachute so the kernels 'pop'.)*I guess that the oil is hot enough. Let's pour the rest of the kernels in.* (Have all of the children toss in their balls. Making sure that everyone is holding onto the parachute, begin waving it slowly.)*The oil is heating up the kernels.* (Wave a little faster.)*Oh look, one kernel popped — another one — oh, two more.* (Wave quickly as all of the kernels begin to 'pop'.)*Oh, all of the popcorn is popping!* (As it is popping, sing this song to the tune of ROW, ROW, ROW YOUR BOAT.)

Pop, pop, pop the corn.
Pop it big and white.
Popping, popping, popping, popping,
Popping 'til it's right.

(Begin to slow the parachute down.) *I think all of the popcorn has popped. Let's be quiet and listen. Do you hear any more kernels popping?* (Answer.)*Thank you for your help. Let's enjoy some popcorn for snack."* (Pretend to eat popcorn.)

BOOKS

TOMI DEPAOLA — *THE POPCORN BOOK*
JANE THAYER — *POPCORN DRAGON*

SAND

FOR OPENERS

BEFORE DISCUSSING SAND, GO TO A LANDSCAPING COMPANY, A NURSERY, OR A CEMENT CONTRACTOR AND BUY SEVERAL GRADES OF SAND RANGING FROM SMOOTH, FINE SAND TO ROUGH, COARSE SAND. PUT EACH TYPE INTO A BUCKET.

BRING THE BUCKETS OF SAND AND SOME PAPER CUPS TO CIRCLE TIME. GIVE EACH CHILD AS MANY PAPER CUPS AS YOU HAVE DIFFERENT TYPES OF SAND. WALK AROUND THE CIRCLE WITH ONE TYPE OF SAND. LET EACH CHILD FEEL THE SAND IN THE BUCKET. THEN POUR A LITTLE SAND INTO ONE OF HIS / HER CUPS. AS YOU ARE WALKING AROUND, TALK ABOUT HOW THE SAND FEELS. DO THIS ACTIVITY WITH ALL OF THE GRADES OF SAND. WHEN EACH CHILD HAS A SAMPLE OF EACH GRADE OF SAND ASK QUESTIONS SUCH AS:

"WHICH TYPE OF SAND DO YOU LIKE BEST? WHY?"

"WHICH ONE WOULD YOU USE TO BUILD A SAND PILE? WHY?"

"ARE THEY ALL THE SAME COLOR?"

EXTENSION: PUT THE SAND IN THE DISCOVERY AREA FOR FURTHER EXPLORATION.

FINGERPLAYS

MY SAND BOX
On sunny days I go to play
In a magic land not far away.
It's filled with sand for castles fair
Or streets that go just everywhere.
And in my truck the sand I load
To fill a hole just down the road.
To find the place is not too hard
It's out the door in my back yard.
Dick Wilmes

SCIENCE

RECIPES

SAND DOLLARS

YOU'LL NEED

Round crackers
Peanut butter
Wheat germ
Parmesan cheese

TO MAKE: Spread peanut butter on the crackers. Let the children sprinkle "sand" on each one by adding wheat germ and parmesan cheese.

FIELD TRIPS

● Spend a day at the beach. Enjoy digging, piling, shaping, and sifting both wet and dry sand. As the children are enjoying their play, ask them questions such as, "Do you like to play in wet or dry sand? How does the sand feel on your skin? What is your favorite thing to play in the sand?"

LANGUAGE GAMES

TELEPHONE

Give each child a toilet paper core. Have him/her hold it up to his/her ear. Quickly go to each child and make a *phone call*. Tell the child one thing that you like to do in the sand. When you have finished making all of your *phone calls*, let each child tell the group the one thing that you had told him/her in the *phone call* and one thing that s/he likes to do in the sand.

At art give the children each another toilet paper roll and a piece of 12" string. Decorate the rolls and then attach to make *telephones*.

FEEL AND GUESS

Before circle time, get one pail of sand and a small object for each child, such as a comb, ball, block, car, etc.

Give one object to each child. Have him/her identify it and then come up to the pail and bury it in the sand. When all of the objects have been buried, call a child to come and feel in the sand with his/her hands until s/he finds an object. Feel all around the object and try to guess what it might be. Then pull the item out and put it on a tray beside the pail. Continue until all of the objects have been found.

CREATIVE
THINKING

Ask the children, *"Where are all of the places that we could find sand?"*

LANGUAGE GAMES

EXPLORING
WET SAND

After the children have had the opportunity to work with dry sand, add water to small tubs of dry sand and let them experience wet sand. Let them touch it. *"Does it feel differently than the dry sand?"* Have them get some wet sand in their hand and squeeze it closed. Count to *'five'* with the children and then have them slowly open their hands. *"What does your sand look like now?"* Put the sand back in the tub. Give each child a small cookie cutter. Let him/her make a design in the sand. Go around and let each child tell what design s/he made.

ACTIVE GAMES

FOLLOW
THE MAZE

Before circle time, make a maze with colored tape in an open area of the room. Get a small paper plate for each child and a bucket of sand.

Give each child a plate. Let him/her scoop a small amount of sand onto his/her plate. When everyone has sand on his/her plate, have him/her walk along the maze while balancing the plate of sand. Have several small brooms and dustpans available, so that if a child should spill sand s/he can readily sweep it up.

EXTENSION:

As the children improve their balancing skills, have them move in different ways along the tape or have them try to balance the plate full of sand on a different part of their body such as the other side of their hand, their head, their foot, and so on.

S
C
I
E
N
C
E

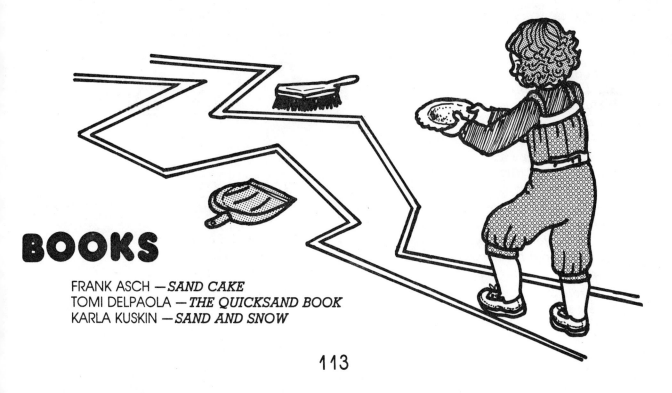

BOOKS

FRANK ASCH — *SAND CAKE*
TOMI DELPAOLA — *THE QUICKSAND BOOK*
KARLA KUSKIN — *SAND AND SNOW*

DIRT

FOR OPENERS

BEFORE CIRCLE TIME, GO TO A NEARBY FIELD, YARD, OR CONSTRUC-
TION SIGHT AND FILL SEVERAL PLASTIC TUBS WITH DIRT (ONE TUB FOR EVERY
THREE OR FOUR CHILDREN). GET SOME TWEEZERS, SPOONS, TONGUE
DEPRESSORS, AND MAGNIFYING GLASSES.

BRING THE TUBS OF DIRT AND UTENSILS TO CIRCLE TIME. BEFORE LETTING
THE CHILDREN EXPLORE THE DIRT, TALK ABOUT THE THINGS THEY MIGHT
FIND WHILE DIGGING THROUGH IT. AS THEY GUESS, WRITE DOWN THEIR
IDEAS.

TALK ABOUT AND SHOW THEM HOW TO EXAMINE THE DIRT BY
SEPARATING IT WITH THE UTENSILS. STRESS THAT THEY MUST BE GENTLE SINCE
THERE MIGHT BE LIVING THINGS IN THE DIRT AND WE MUST NOT HURT THEM.
HAVE THE CHILDREN SIT IN SMALL CLUSTERS AND BEGIN EXAMINING THE
DIRT. AS THEY FIND THINGS IN THE DIRT, HAVE THEM TELL THE GROUP.

WHEN THEY ARE FINISHED, COMPARE WHAT THEY FOUND TO WHAT THEY
THOUGHT THEY WOULD FIND.

FINGERPLAYS

DIRT

Dirt comes in colors,
Black, red, and brown.
It makes a home for animals,
Living in the ground.

Worms, snakes, ants, and bugs
Live beneath my shoe.
If there wasn't dirt between us
I wouldn't know what to do.

Dirt helps the tree to stand
Stately green and tall.
If it wasn't for our friend the dirt
I'm sure those trees would fall.

Dirt feeds the plants you know,
Minerals and nutrients too.
I'll eat my vegetables,
And leave the dirt for you!
                        Dick Wilmes

DRY DIRT, WET DIRT

Dry dirt, wet dirt,
Oh, what fun,
Sitting in the backyard,
Playing in the sun.
Dry dirt is dusty
Wet dirt is mud.
Drop the wet dirt on the ground
And hear it go thud.
                        Dick Wilmes

RECIPES

DIRT

YOU'LL NEED

Raisins
Dates
Prunes
Black olives

TO MAKE: While talking about dirt, enjoy black and brown foods. To make the dates and prunes more tasty, pit and then stuff with cream cheese and top with a walnut or pecan.

LANGUAGE GAMES

MEMORY
Have a large tray of items that are found in and on top of the dirt; bark, leaves, acorns, pine cones, roots, seeds, twigs, flowers, fruit, etc. Hold up each item and let a child name it. Then pass the tray around and let each child take one item off of it. When each child has an item, have him/her hold up the item, name it, and then hide it behind his/her back. When all of the items are hidden, say to the children, *"I'm looking for an acorn. Everybody point to the child who's hiding it."* If the child that is being pointed at has the *'acorn'*, s/he holds it up. If s/he does not have an *'acorn'*, have him/her shake his/her head, *"No'*. When all of the items have been identified, pass the tray around the circle to collect the items.

At art make *'nature'* collages.

CREATIVE
THINKING
Have the children name as many things as they can think of that are made out of wood.

TALK ABOUT
Read this poem.

BUGS
1, 2, 3 — There's a bug on me!
Where did he go?
I don't know.

After you have read the poem, talk about all of the places that the bug could have gone.

S
C
I
E
N
C
E

LANGUAGE GAMES

EXPLORING DIRT
Take a walk to a nearby field. Let each child have a spoon and a small tub. Each child should dig up some dirt to fill the tub. Walk back to school.

The children should sit in the circle time area. Give each child a paper towel and let him/her pour the dirt onto it. Have several magnifying glasses, blunt knives, and tweezers available. Examine the dirt closely. (Because they have done a similar activity in small groups, they should know how to use the utensils.) As the children find things in the dirt, have them tell the others. Make a list of the things as the children call them out.

EXTENSION:
Once the children have examined the dirt, have them pour it back into their tub. Walk around the circle with a pitcher of water and help each child add water to his/her tub. Let them stir the water into the tub. *"What is happening to the dirt? What is another word for wet dirt?"*

ACTIVE GAMES

CREATIVE MOVEMENT
Have the children pretend that they are things associated with the soil:
- Sway like trees in the wind.
- Fall like trees being chopped down.
- Crawl like ants.
- Sprout like a newly developing plant.
- Swirl like a leaf falling to the ground in the wind.
- Curl up like an acorn.
- Roll like a pinecone tumbling down the hill.

ARM DANCING
Roll out a long sheet of butcher paper. Have the children sit all around it. Give each child a black and brown crayon. Play music and let the children 'crayon' the paper to the beat of the music. Change the tempo several times, so that the children can 'arm dance' at different speeds. Continue 'arm dancing' until the sheet has become the color of dirt. Hang your mural for all to enjoy.

EXTENSION:
Use the 'dirt' as the ground for a more extensive mural. Have the children add trees, bugs, flowers, and other items which live and grow in the dirt.

BOOKS

JUDI BARRETT — *I HATE TO TAKE A BATH*
JUDITH VIGNA — *THE LITTLE BOY WHO LOVED DIRT AND ALMOST BECAME A SUPERSLOB*

PLANTING

FOR OPENERS

BEGIN SEVERAL CIRCLE TIMES BY PLANTING. ONE DAY PLANT BULBS, ONE DAY SEEDS, AND ANOTHER DAY CUTTINGS WHICH HAVE BEEN RECENTLY ROOTED. (SEVERAL WEEKS BEFOREHAND, TAKE CUTTINGS FROM TWO OR THREE DIFFERENT TYPES OF PLANTS. ROOT ONE CUTTING FOR EACH CHILD.)

ON THE DAY YOU PLANT THE CUTTINGS, GIVE EACH CHILD A ROOTED STEM. LOOK CAREFULLY AT THE ROOTS WHICH HAVE BEGUN TO SPROUT. HAVE MAGNIFYING GLASSES AVAILABLE FOR CLOSER EXAMINATION. MARK EACH CHILD'S CONTAINER AND PUT ALL OF THEM NEAR THE WINDOW. CARE FOR THESE PLANTS BY WATERING THEM AS NEEDED AND TURNING THEM SO EACH SIDE GETS ENOUGH SUN.

IT IS FUN TO PLANT GRASS SEED ON POTATO SLICES. GIVE ONE SLICE TO EACH CHILD. LET HIM / HER SPRINKLE GRASS SEED ON TOP OF THE POTATO. MARK EACH CHILD'S POTATO. PUT THEM IN A SHALLOW BAKING PAN AND SET IT IN THE SUNLIGHT. KEEP MOIST, BY ADDING A LITTLE WATER EACH DAY. WATCH CAREFULLY AND SEE WHAT BEGINS TO GROW FROM THE POTATOES.

BRING BULBS AND PLANTING ACCESSORIES TO THE CIRCLE TIME. BEFORE ACTUALLY PLANTING THE BULBS, TALK ABOUT THEM. GIVE EACH CHILD A BULB AND NOTE ITS SHAPE, SIZE, TEXTURE, SMELL, ETC. CUT ONE BULB OPEN AND LOOK AT THE INSIDE, WHAT DO YOU SEE? PLANT THE BULBS. AFTER EACH CHILD HAS PLANTED A BULB, MARK HIS / HER NAME ON THE CONTAINER AND SET UP A SCHEDULE FOR CARING FOR IT.

FINGERPLAYS

PLANTING

I took a little seed one day
About a month ago.
I put it in a pot of dirt,
In hopes that it would grow.

I poured a little water
To make the soil right.
I set the pot upon the sill,
Where the sun would give it light.

I checked the pot most every day,
And turned it once or twice.
With a little care and water
I helped it grow so nice.
                    Dick Wilmes

RECIPES

SPROUTS

YOU'LL NEED

Mung bean seeds or alfalfa seeds
A glass jar covered with a piece of
    cheese cloth

TO MAKE: Sprouts grow quickly and are
fun to watch. Have the children fill their
jar about $\frac{1}{16}$ full of seeds. Fill the jar
with warm water. Rinse them several
times. Fill again with warm water and
put the jar in a warm, dark place overnight. Every morning rinse the seeds
with warm water. Pour out excess
water. Keep in a warm, dark place. Do
this for 3-4 days. Soon the seeds will
sprout. When grown keep them
refrigerated. Enjoy eating the sprouts
on sandwiches, salads, or plain. They
will last for about 1½ to 2 weeks.

FIELD TRIPS

● Take a slow walk around the block or through a nearby field. As you are walking, look for all types of plants and flowers. Do you see any dandelions? Remember,
weeds are plants too.

LANGUAGE GAMES

FLOWER GARDEN

Cut 12" x 4" strips of lightweight cardboard. (At least one for each child.) Fold each strip in half so that it forms a tent. Use stickers or cut a picture of a flower out of a magazine or catalogue and glue it onto one side of each card. Play a variety of games with the flower cards.

• Pass a card to each child. Have them look at their card and then sit on it. Say, *"Those children with yellow flowers, stand your card in front of you."* Continue with all of the colors. When all of the flowers are displayed, have the children one by one bring their flower to you. When they bring it up, have them say to the group, *"I'm putting a 'red' flower in the garden."* As s/he says this, have him/her put the flower card in front of you. Soon all of the flowers will make a colorful *'flower garden'*.

• Have the children switch cards and once again look carefully at them. Stand the cards in front of them. Say, *"Those children with pictures of 'red' flowers, stand up; those with flowers having four leaves, hold up four fingers; those with flowers having long stems, make yourself as long as you can."* and so on.

FELT BOARD FUN

Make felt pieces that show the growth of a flower. Have a bulb, seed, cuttings, roots, stem, leaves, and a flower. Put the parts of the flower on the felt board. Name each part. Talk about the order in which the flower will grow. As you discuss this, have a child come up and put the appropriate part on the *'growing'* plant.

At art drizzle glue onto green construction paper. Then sprinkle flower seeds along the glue. When dry, shake off the excess seeds. Print what type of seeds were used.

ENJOYING FLOWERS

Cut out large pictures of flowers. Mount them on construction paper. Hold them up one at a time. Have the children identify the colors in each of the pictures. Talk about what is *'pretty'* about each flower that is pictured. Help the children begin to note detail and verbally express that detail.

SCIENCE

119

ACTIVE GAMES

CREATIVE MOVEMENT

Have the children pretend that they are little seeds growing into beautiful flowers. "*It is Spring and time to do planting. After the ground has been prepared, holes are dug to put the seeds into.* (Have the children kneel down and curl up like a seed.) *During the next several weeks, the warm sun heats the ground and seeds. Water brings nourishment. Soon the root begins to grow and wiggle through the soil.* (Have the children begin to uncurl.) *Soon a stem begins to come through the ground and grows tall.* (Have the children squat.) *Leaves sprout out and the stem continues to grow.* (The arms can be leaves and the children can be almost standing straight.) *The warm sun and rain continue to help the flower grow. Soon a bud is on the flower and it begins to open up.* (Have the children stand straight with their heads tucked down.) *The bud blooms and the flower is beautiful.*" (Have all of the children stand up straight, arms out, and heads up with bright smiles on their faces.)

BOOKS

HELENE JORDAN — *HOW A SEED GROWS*
PATRICIA LAUBER — *SEEDS*
GENE ZION — *THE PLANT SITTER*

TREES

FOR OPENERS

TREES CAN BE USED FOR A VARIETY OF THINGS AND ACTIVITIES. ASK THE CHILDREN WHAT THEY DO WITH TREES. DO THEIR MOMS AND DADS USE TREES? HOW? READ THE BOOK *THE GIVING TREE* BY SHEL SILVERSTEIN. AFTER READING THE BOOK, DISCUSS THE WAYS THE PERSON IN THE STORY USED HIS TREE AS COMPARED TO THE WAYS THE CHILDREN AND THEIR FAMILIES USE THEIRS.

FINGERPLAYS

OAK TREE
Here is an oak tree, straight and tall
And here are its branches wide.
Here is a nest of twigs and moss,
With three little birds inside.
The breezes blow, and the little leaves play,
But the branches hold the nest
As they sway and bob and rock
So the little birds can rest.

THE TREE
I am a tall tree
I reach toward the sky,
Where bright stars twinkle
And clouds float by.
My branches toss high
As the wild winds blow,
And they bend forward,
So full of snow.
When they sway gently
I like it best.
Then I rock the birds to sleep
In their nest.

TREES
Elm trees stretch and stretch so wide,
Their limbs reach out on every side.
Pine trees stretch and stretch so high.
They nearly reach up to the sky.
Willows droop and droop so low,
Their branches sweep the ground below.

RECIPES

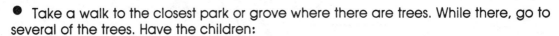

TREES

YOU'LL NEED

A bunch of fresh broccoli

TO MAKE: Wash the bunch of broccoli.
Break a piece of broccoli for each child.
Serve them so they are standing up
and look like a grove of trees.

FIELD TRIPS

● Take a walk to the closest park or grove where there are trees. While there, go to
several of the trees. Have the children:

- Feel the bark.
- Look at the leaves.
- Look for any animal homes.
- Hug the tree and see how far around their arms go.
- Decide which is taller, the child or the tree?

LANGUAGE GAMES

LEAVES

Collect a variety of different size leaves. Give one to each
child. Say, *"Anyone who has a large leaf, hold it up high."*
Have all of the children come up to the front with their leaf.
Have them hold up their leaves again. Have all of the
children who are sitting, look carefully at the leaves and
pick out the leaf that is the largest.

Repeat the activity for the smallest leaf. Then have the
children stand in a line holding the leaves from largest to
smallest.

At art iron leaves between pieces of wax paper.

LANGUAGE GAMES

TREE HOMES — Say to the children, *"What animals make their homes in trees?"* (Bird-nest, spider-web, bee-hive, squirrel-hole, caterpiller-coccoon) If possible, have examples or pictures of each type of home. As the children say a home, show them the example.

At art dip string into liquid starch. Arrange the string into a spider web on a piece of wax paper. Let dry overnight. In the morning the children can hang them on the *'special tree'* described in SCHOOL BEGINS.

FRUIT FROM TREES — Many of our fruits grow on trees — apples, oranges, grapefruit, lemons, limes, and so on. Make the different fruits out of construction paper, having two or three for each child. Punch a hole at the tip of each piece of fruit and loop a piece of yarn through it. Pass the fruits out. Have each child name the fruit s/he has, then go and hang them on the *'special tree'* in your room (see SCHOOL BEGINS for construction.)

EXTENSION:
Have pieces of these fruits for snack.

FELT BOARD FUN — Make a large felt tree and three different sizes of apples, leaves, birds, nests, and pinecones. Enjoy a variety of activities with the children.
- Match the ones that go together.
- Put each category in order by size.
- Mix and match the pieces and tell stories using the pieces for props.

EXTENSION:
Using the tree and objects, give directions to the children stressing the position words. For example:
"Eric, put your apple under the tree."
"Greg, hang your leaf high in the tree."

SCIENCE

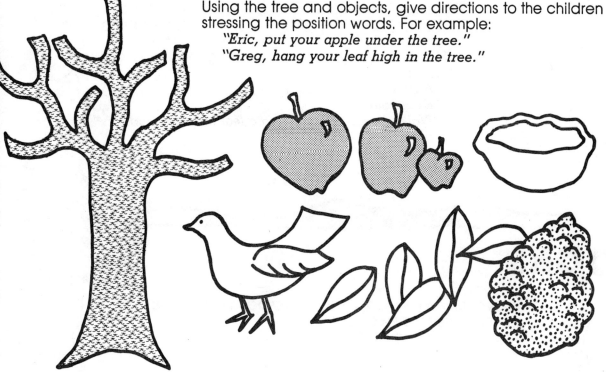

123

ACTIVE GAMES

CREATIVE MOVEMENT

Have the children pretend that they are 'trees' being blown by the wind. The teacher is the 'wind'. Blow softly, blow hard. Vary the strength of the 'wind' and have the children move their bodies accordingly.

EXTENSION:

When the children know how it feels to be tossed around by the 'wind', talk about the rain that is approaching. *"Scott and his friends are outside playing. There is no rain; a little breeze is blowing; the branches on the trees are hardly moving.* (Have the children wave in the breeze.) *Scott's grandmother just called on the telephone and said that it had begun to rain at her house and that soon it would start at Scott's house. Scott's mom came outside and told Scott's friends to go right home and that Scott should come inside because a big storm was on its way. Sure enough, soon after everybody was inside, the wind began to blow harder.* (The teacher should blow harder and the children wave like the trees in the stronger breeze.) *The wind got stronger* (The children move faster.) *and soon the rain came. It rained a long time. The trees and other plants were getting a good drink of water. Scott sat by the window and watched the rain. The trees were soaked with water. Puddles were forming on the sidewalk. Scott could see mud in the garden. The rain began to let up. The wind calmed down.* (The children can wave more slowly.) *Finally the rain was over. The breeze continued to blow, drying off many of the things that the rain had gotten so wet."*

Once the story is completed, ask the children, *"What things around Scott's house did the breeze help to dry off after the rain?"*

SIMON SAYS

When the children are outside, have them pick up a leaf that has fallen from a tree. Take it inside and then bring it with them to circle time.

Simon should give directions using the leaves as props.

Simon says:

"Hold your leaf up high."
"Hide your leaf."
"Walk in a circle balancing a leaf on your head."

Continue.

BOOKS

MAY GARELICK & BARBARA BRENNER — *THE TREMENDOUS TREE BOOK*
VIRGINIA POULET — *BLUE BUG FINDS A FRIEND*
SHEL SILVERSTEIN — *THE GIVING TREE*
JANICE UDRY — *A TREE IS NICE*

DINOSAURS

FOR OPENERS

DINOSAURS ARE MONSTERS OF THE PAST. THE WORD DINOSAUR MEANS "TERRIBLE LIZARD". THERE WERE MANY TYPES OF DINOSAURS, HOWEVER, THESE SIX ARE THE MOST RECOGNIZABLE:

- BRONTOSAURUS MEANS "THUNDER LIZARD". IT WEIGHED AS MUCH AS TEN ELEPHANTS AND ATE ONLY PLANTS, THUS IT WAS A VEGETARIAN.
- PTERODACTYL MEANS "WING-FINGERED". IT HAD VERY LARGE WINGS THAT HELPED IT FLY THROUGH THE AIR. IT SWOOPPED DOWN OUT OF THE SKY LIKE A KITE DIVING TO THE GROUND.
- STEGOSAURUS HAD HARD, BONY PLATES ALONG ITS BACK. HIS TAIL HAD FOUR LONG SPIKES AT ITS TIP. THEY WERE USED FOR DEFENSE AGAINST ENEMIES.
- TYRANNOSAURUS WAS "KING OF THE LIZARDS". HE WAS AS LONG AS A FIRE TRUCK AND HAD TEETH LIKE BIG KNIVES.
- TRACHODON HAD A BILL LIKE A DUCK. EACH BILL HAD ABOUT 2000 TEETH IN IT.
- TRICERATOPS WAS A "THREE HORNED" LIZARD. IT WAS BUILT LIKE AN ARMY TANK.

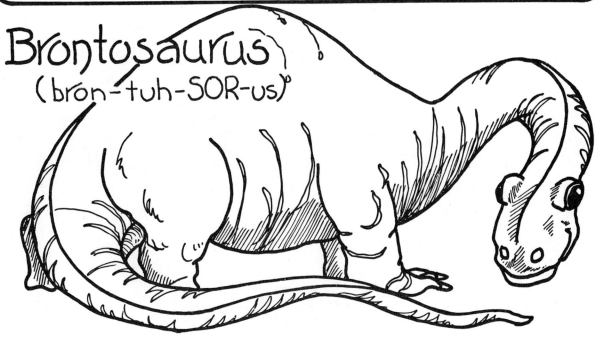

Brontosaurus
(bron-tuh-SOR-us)

SCIENCE

Pterodactyl
(ter-oh-DAK-til)

Stegosaurus
(STEG-oh-SOR-us)

Tyrannosaurus
(ti-RAN-oh-SOR-us)

Triceratops
(try-SER-a-tops)

126

FINGERPLAYS

ILL-MANNERED DINOSAURS

Never go to lunch with a dinosaur.
They're a mean, foul, nasty group.
They burp and slurp and never sit down
They are likely to step in your soup.

The biggest are called vegetarians,
Which means they eat grass and trees.
But when you're longer than a school bus,
You can eat whatever you please.

The rest are called carnivores
Which means they eat mostly meat
If there aren't enough hot dogs to go around
They probably will chomp on your feet.

And when it comes time to clear the plates
They'll try to sneak away.
Instead of helping with the dishes,
They'll try to go out to play.
Dick Wilmes

Trachodon
(TRAK-oh-don)

RECIPES

DINOSAUR SOUP

YOU'LL NEED

3 to 4 soup bones
3 quarts of water
1 large onion
Celery leaves
Chopped parsley
4 t. allspice
4 pepper corns
3 bay leaves
About 4 cups of vegetables such as
   carrots, celery, cabbage, peas,
   beans, corn, potatoes.
1 large can of tomatoes
⅓ cup of barley
Salt to taste

TO MAKE: Get beef soup bones from the butcher. When making this soup you can pretend they are "dinosaur bones." Brown the meaty bones in a large kettle. Cover the bones with water and bring to a boil for about 15 minutes. Skim the top if necessary. Lower the heat and simmer for about 2 hours with the seasonings. Remove the bones. Put the meat in the soup. Add all of the vegetables and cook for about 20 minutes or until the vegetables are tender.
from COME AND GET IT
by Kathleen Baxter

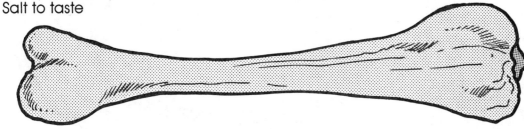

LANGUAGE GAMES

IDENTIFYING DINOSAURS

Using the dinosaur pictures above, make at least one dinosaur card for each child. Pass the dinosaur cards out. Say, *"I'm looking for pictures of a brontosaurus. The brontosaurus weighed as much as ten elephants and ate only plants. Those who have brontosaurus cards stand up and make yourself look very large!"* Go around the circle and say the names of all of the children who are pretending to be a brontosaurus. *"Amy is a brontosaurus. Ian is a brontosaurus"* and so on. Continue by identifying the other five types of dinosaurs.

SPINNER FUN

Cut a large circle out of posterboard and divide it into six sections. Put a picture of a different dinosaur in each section. Attach a spinner to the middle of the circle with a heavy-duty brad.

Let one child come up and flick the spinner. Have the other children call out the name of the dinosaur to which the spinner points.

EXTENSION

Let the children pretend to be that type of dinosaur.

CREATIVE THINKING

Ask the children, *"If you were a dinosaur, what types of games would you play?"*

128

ACTIVE GAMES

DINOSAUR DANCE

Punch a hole in each of the dinosaur cards that you made above. Hook a long piece of yarn in each one so that the children can wear them around their necks.

Give each child a dinosaur card. The children should begin to dance when the music starts, pretending to be the dinosaur on their card. When the music stops, all of the children should freeze and begin dancing again when the music restarts.

VARIATION:

Dance as directed above, but just before you restart the music to continue dancing, have the children exchange cards and pretend to be a different type of dinosaur.

PARACHUTE PLAY

Let the children move the parachute (sheet) as if it were different types of dinosaurs. For example, the children can pretend to be the pterodactyl by standing, letting the parachute float through the sky like his large wings, dive for something on the ground, and then take off again. The stegosaurus had a tail which it used for defense. Let the parachute be the tail moving back and forth protecting the stegosaurus.

SCIENCE

BOOKS

ALIKI — *MY VISIT TO THE DINOSAURS*
PEGGY PARRISH — *DINOSAUR TIME*
MIRIAM YOUNG — *IF I RODE A DINOSAUR*

WEATHER

FOR OPENERS

MAKE A WEATHER CHART FOR A MONTH. GET A LARGE PIECE OF POSTER-
BOARD AND MAKE IT INTO A CALENDAR. THEN MAKE A VARIETY OF
WEATHER SYMBOLS WHICH WILL FIT INTO THE DAILY BOXES. PUT THE SYM-
BOLS IN A BOX.

WINDY
RAINY
CLOUDY
SUNNY
SNOWY

DURING CIRCLE TIME EACH DAY TAKE SEVERAL MINUTES TO DISCUSS THE
WEATHER. HAVE A CHILD PUT THE APPROPRIATE WEATHER SYMBOL/S ON
THE CHART. AS THE DAYS GO ON, YOU WILL BE ABLE TO COUNT HOW
MANY RAINY, SUNNY OR OTHER TYPES OF DAYS THERE HAVE BEEN.

FINGERPLAYS

SUMMER SUN
You see me in the sky above,
On a summer's day.
I am a welcome friend of yours,
When you go out to play.

I heat the ground with rays so warm,
And help the flowers grow.
But if you're not careful on sunny days,
I might burn your skin, you know.
Dick Wilmes

WHEN THE COLD WIND BLOWS
When cold winds blow,
And bring on the snow,
At night what I like most,
Is to climb in bed
And hide my head,
And sleep as warm as toast.
"SHHHHHHHHHHH — Good Night!"

RAIN
From big black clouds
The raindrops fell,
Drip, drip, drip one day,
Until the bright sunlight changed them
Into a rainbow gay.

RAINY DAY FUN
Slip on your raincoat.
Pull up your galoshes.
Wade in puddles.
Make splishes and sploshes.

THUNDERSTORM
Boom, bang, boom, bang!
Rumpety, lumpety, bump!
Zoom, zam, zoom, zam!
Rustles and bustles
And swishes and zings!
What wonderful noises
A thunderstorm brings.

RECIPES

SNOW

YOU'LL NEED

Your favorite pudding
Coconut

TO MAKE: Make your favorite pudding with the children. Just before serving, let each child drizzle "snow" on his/her pudding by sprinkling coconut on the top.

FIELD TRIPS

● Take a walk after it rains. (Be sure everyone is properly dressed.) Enjoy the puddles, overflowing gutters, and swirls of water caught by the sewers. Look in the puddles. Does anyone see his/her reflection? How deep are the puddles? Look up in the sky. Do you see any clouds, the sun, and possibly a rainbow? What colors are in the rainbow? Touch the water. How does it feel?

SCIENCE

LANGUAGE GAMES

TALK ABOUT   You want your children to be thinking about, observing, and drawing conclusions about the weather. Ask questions such as:

"What do you do when it rains?"
"How does the sky look when it rains?"
"How do you feel when the wind is blowing very hard?"
"What do you do when you are too hot?" "Too cold?"

LANGUAGE GAMES

CREATIVE THINKING

Read this poem to your children and then ask them, *"Why didn't the rain get on the person?"* You may have to read the poem again or you may have to encourage the children to use their imagination since the *'answer'* is not in the poem.

> *RAIN*
> *Rain on green grass,*
> *And rain on the tree,*
> *Rain on the rooftop,*
> *But not on me!*

SEASONS CHANGE

Read the book THE BIG SNOW by Hader and Hader. Talk about how all of the animals are getting ready for winter. As you read, note how the weather is changing from lovely fall weather to snowy, windy winter weather.

EXTENSION:

Talk about how people get ready for winter. What do they do to protect their homes, to change their clothes, to winterize their cars and other vehicles, to change their tools and machines, and so on.

WEATHER CUBE

Get a square-shaped box. Find six different pictures of weather — windy, snowy, rainy, foggy, cloudy, and sunny. Glue one picture onto each side of the box. Cover the pictues with clear contact.

At circle time, roll the cube to a child. Have the child tell the others what type of weather is facing up on the cube and what s/he likes to do in that type of weather. Have that child roll the cube to another child. Continue in this manner.

132

ACTIVE GAMES

PARACHUTE PLAY

Bring a parachute (sheet) and several tennis balls to circle time. The parachute is going to represent the ocean, the balls will be the ships, and the children will be the wind blowing up a storm.

Have the children hold the parachute with the balls in the center. Just have them gently bounce the balls around on the parachute without having any of them fall off. Once you feel that they have control of the parachute with the balls on it, begin the story.

"The sailors woke up after a good night of rest. When they looked at the sky, they noticed very dark clouds off in the distance. Up on the deck the wind was beginning to blow. (Have the children blow slightly and begin to wave the parachute. The balls do not start to jump.) *The sailors knew that soon they would be in the midst of a storm. Soon the wind got stronger and the ships began to rock back and forth.* (Have the children blow a little harder and the balls begin to bounce.) *The rain started to fall, so the sailors went for shelter. Soon the wind was blowing harder and harder. The ships were being tossed by the waves of the ocean* (Blow hard and have the balls bounce higher.) *The sailors were afraid for they had never been out in such a fierce storm.* (Keep the balls bouncing but do not let them fly off of the parachute.) *After several hours they heard the captain say over the intercom, 'The storm has passed. Come up on deck now. It is still windy, but it is safe.'* (Have the wind calm down, the parachute slow down, and the balls simply rock back and forth.) *The sailors were happy that they and their ships were safe."*

WEATHER HUNT

Get a 12" x 12" piece of posterboard for each child in the group. Draw a simple picture of a different type of weather on each piece. Cut each piece in four pieces.

At circle time give one piece from each puzzle to each player. Mix up the remaining pieces and lay them down end to end in *'trail fashion'*. The first child walks down the *'trail'* until s/he finds a piece to his/her puzzle. S/he picks it up and the next child begins down the *'trail'* searching for a second piece to his/her puzzle. Continue until all of the children have two pieces. Then starting with the first child repeat the search until each of the children has found all four of their puzzle pieces. Let them put all of the pieces together to form their *'weather puzzle.'*

EXTENSION:

Put the variety of weather puzzles on the manipulative shelf. Encourage the children to talk about the various types of weather as they put the puzzles together.

S C I E N C E

BOOKS

FRANKLYN BRANLEY — *SUNSHINE MAKES SEASONS*
AILEEN FISHER — *I LIKE WEATHER*

SNOW

FOR OPENERS

HAVE THE CHILDREN BRING THEIR MITTENS TO CIRCLE TIME. EACH CHILD SHOULD KEEP ONE MITTEN AND PUT THE MATE IN A BOX. HAVE THE CHILDREN PASS THEIR REMAINING MITTENS TO THE CHILD SITTING NEXT TO THEM. NOW EVERYONE SHOULD PUT ON A MITTEN. HOLD UP ONE OF THE MITTENS FROM THE BOX. SAY, "LOOK AT THE MITTEN YOU ARE WEARING. IF THE ONE I'M HOLDING MATCHES THE ONE YOU ARE WEARING, COME HERE AND WE'LL MAKE A PAIR." CONTINUE UNTIL EVERYONE HAS A PAIR OF MITTENS. PASS THE BOX AROUND THE CIRCLE AND HAVE THE CHILDREN PUT ONE MITTEN BACK INTO IT. HAVE THE CHILDREN PASS THEIR OTHER MITTEN TO ANOTHER CHILD AND PLAY THE GAME AGAIN.

FINGERPLAYS

MITTEN WEATHER

Thumbs in the thumb place,
Fingers all together
This is the song we sing
During mitten weather.

WALKING IN THE SNOW

Let's go walking in the snow,
Walking, walking on tiptoe.
Lift your one foot way up high.
Then the other to keep it dry.
All around the yard we skip.
Watch your step, or you might slip.

CHUBBY LITTLE SNOWMAN

A chubby little snowman had a carrot nose.
Along came a bunny, and what do you suppose?
That hungry little bunny, looking for his lunch,
Ate the snowman's carrot nose,
Nibble, nibble, crunch!

SNOWFLAKES

Many little snowflakes
Falling through the air,
Resting on the steeple
And trees everywhere.
Covering roofs and fences,
Capping every post,
Covering the hillside,
Where we like to coast.

RECIPES

CUSTARD
YOU'LL NEED
2 to 4 eggs
2 T. honey
2 cups milk
1 t. vanilla
¼ t. nutmeg

TO MAKE: Beat the eggs. Add the honey and beat again. Mix everything together. Pour the mixture into custard dishes. Place the dishes in a pan with ½ inch of water. Bake at 350 degrees for 45 minutes. Insert a knife into the custard. If it comes out clean, it is done. Makes 4.

from COME AND GET IT
by Kathleen Baxter

FRUITY SLUSH
YOU'LL NEED
Orange juice

TO MAKE: Freeze orange juice in ice cube trays. Put the frozen cubes into a plastic bag to store. Put 3 to 6 of these cubes into the blender. Turn the blender on and off until the cubes reach a snowy consistency. Spoon the slush into a paper cup and serve.
from A FAMILY AFFAIR: SNACKS
by Aviva Croll

FIELD TRIPS

• Visit the local hardware store and look at the different machines and materials used to shovel and control snow. Have the hardware clerk show the children the special melting compound, snow shovels, snow blowers, hand driven plows, and other things s/he keeps in stock during the winter months.

As you go back to school, look for people using some of the materials and equipment. Where are they using them, on their sidewalk, driveway, porch? What are they using? Does their job look hard or easy? Why?

LANGUAGE GAMES

EXPLORING SNOW

Give each child a clear dish. Go outside and have him/her fill the dish with snow. Bring the children back inside to the circle time area. Let each child look carefully at his/her snow. Encourage the children to touch the snow, smell it, listen to it. Have magnifying glass available for even closer examination. As the children are exploring the snow, make a list of their comments. When you have finished, read the list to them. Post it for all of the parents to enjoy.

LANGUAGE GAMES

CREATIVE
THINKING

Bring a tray of white foods to circle time — coconut, cream cheese, cottage cheese, bananas, yogurt, vanilla pudding, popcorn, cauliflower, and so on. Ask the children, *"What is the same about all of the things on my tray?"* Let them answer. Encourage them to really think beyond the two obvious answers, *"They are all foods."* and *"They are all white."* Then talk about which of the foods look like snow. What makes them look like snow?

EXTENSION:

Let the children pretend that they are eating *'snow'* by sampling the foods that look like snow.

SNOW SAFETY

Discuss why the streets and sidewalks can be especially dangerous during the winter season. Knowing that they are more hazardous, what should the children do to be safer? What things should they watch out for?

Playing in the snow can be lots of fun. The children should remember to come inside when they get too cold and/or wet. Talk about all of the *'snow fun'* you have. As you discuss each game, talk about the safety involved.

GETTING
DRESSED

Getting dressed for snow is often a laborious task because of all of the extra clothes. Have each of the children bring their snow clothes to circle time. Talk about the order in which they should put their clothes on and how to fasten the different clasps. Then get dressed together, talking as you proceed. When everyone is ready, go for a walk in the snow.

EXTENSION:

Before putting on all of the winter clothes, read the story A SNOWY DAY by Ezra Jack Keats. Get dressed. Let each child have a stick. As they are walking, they can pretend to be the boy in the story.

ACTIVE GAMES

CATCHING SNOWFLAKES
Take a walk while it is snowing. Give each child a piece of dark construction paper. Have them catch snowflakes on the paper. As the snowflakes are 'caught', have the children look carefully at their designs. *"Are the designs all the same or are they different? Do the snowflakes last a long time or do they melt quickly? Why do they melt?"*
Make snowflakes at art.

CREATIVE MOVEMENT
After the children have been out in several types of snow falls, have them pretend to be 'snowflakes'. Talk about how snow floats from the sky, what the wind does to the snowflakes, and how the flakes land on the ground. Start by being snowflakes gently falling from the sky. A winter wind comes howling along and begins to swirl the snow around and around, jumping and whirling. The snow stops falling, the wind calms down, and all is peaceful.

BLOWING SNOWFLAKES
Pretend that ping-pong balls are 'snowflakes'. Give each child one. Play a recording of *"FROSTY THE SNOWMAN"*. When the music starts, have the children blow their ping-pong balls around the floor like 'snowflakes' being blown around in the wind. When the music stops, the wind has died down and the children should pick up their 'snowflakes' and hold them very quietly.

PASS THE SNOWBALL
Sing this song to the tune of *LONDON BRIDGE IS FALLING DOWN* . As you sing, pass a styrofoam ball around the circle.

Pass the snowball 'round and 'round,
'Round and 'round, 'round and 'round.
Pass the snowball 'round and 'round,
All around the circle.

The child holding the ball when the song is over, begins passing the 'snowball' when the singing starts again.

BOOKS

FRANKLYN BRANLEY — *SNOW IS FALLING*
RAYMOND BRIGGS — *THE SNOWMAN*
EZRA JACK KEATS — *THE SNOWY DAY*
ALVIN TRESSELT — *WHITE SNOW, BRIGHT SNOW*

SKY

FOR OPENERS

MAKE A 'SKY CUBE'. GET A SQUARE-SIDED BOX ABOUT FOUR TO EIGHT IN-CHES IN DIAMETER OR CUT DOWN A PAPER MILK CARTON OR JUICE CAR-TON. FIND PICTURES OF THE NATURAL THINGS FOUND IN THE SKY SUCH AS STARS, A SUN, A MOON, CLOUDS, A RAINBOW, AND A PLANET. TAPE ONE PICTURE ON EACH SIDE OF THE CUBE. COVER THE PICTURES WITH CLEAR ADHESIVE FOR DURABILITY.

ROLL THE CUBE TO A CHILD. HAVE HIM / HER SHOW THE TOP PICTURE TO THE GROUP. HAVE THEM QUIETLY IDENTIFY THE PICTURE. NOW HAVE THE CHILD ROLL THE CUBE TO ANOTHER CHILD. THE NEXT CHILD THEN HOLDS THE CUBE AND ALL OF THE CHILDREN NAME THAT PICTURE. ROLL AGAIN AND AGAIN.

EXTENSION: WALK OUTSIDE AND LOOK UP IN THE SKY. IDENTIFY ALL OF THE THINGS THE CHILDREN SEE, SOME WILL BE NATURAL AND SOME MAY BE MAN-MADE.

FINGERPLAYS

THE SUN
Over there the sun gets up
And marches all the day.
At noon it stands right overhead,
And at night it goes away.

CLOUDS
What's fluffy white and floats up high,
Like piles of ice cream in the sky?
And when the wind blows hard and strong,
What very gently floats along?
What seems to have just lots of fun,
Peek-a-booing with the sun?
When you look up in the big blue sky,
What are these things you see floating by?
(When you have finished saying this riddle, have the children shout out the answer.)

THE STARS
I watch the stars come out at night.
I wonder where they get their light.
I don't think they will ever fall,
So I'll reach up and pick them all.

STARS
At night when I see the twinkling stars,
And a great big smiling moon,
My Mommy tucks me into bed,
And sings a good-night tune.

RECIPES

SUN TEA

YOU'LL NEED

A quart of water
Several bags of herb tea
Fresh lemon (optional)
Honey (optional)

TO MAKE: Place the water and tea in a covered quart container and set in the sun for several hours. Add lemon or honey to taste. Pour in glasses over lots of ice.
from COME AND GET IT
by Kathleen Baxter

SUNSHINE SNACK

YOU'LL NEED

Hard boiled eggs
Saltine crackers

TO MAKE: Peel the hard boiled eggs. Cut them in thick slices so the yolk is round. Put each "sun" on a cracker.

LANGUAGE GAMES

FUN IN THE SUN

During free play, make a book with the children about things that they do in the sun. First cut the pages into the shape of suns from yellow construction paper. Have the children look through magazines, newspapers, and travel brochures for activities that people are enjoying in the sun. Cut out the pictures and glue them onto the pages. Have the children dictate what they would like to say about each picture. You can write what they say as they dictate. When the book is completed, bring it to the circle time and read it to the group. Put FUN IN THE SUN on the book shelf for the children to read on their own.

MEMORY

Cut out various natural and man-made objects that function in the sky — sun, moon, airplane, rocket, kite, paper airplane, balloon, and so on. Hang these from the ceiling in the circle time area. Have all of the children lie on their backs and look up at the 'sky'. Have the first child say, *"I'm looking up at the sky and I see the moon."* The second child says, *"I'm looking in the sky and I see the moon and the sun."* Continue around the circle having the remaining children try to repeat the previous objects and name a new one of his/her own.

SCIENCE

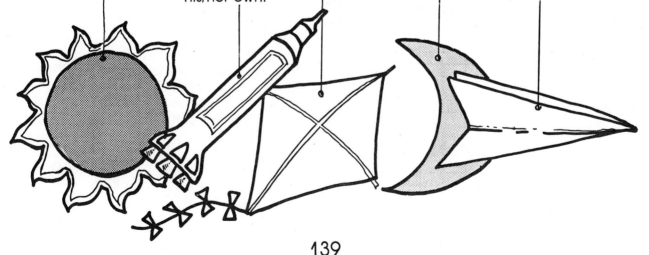

LANGUAGE GAMES

IT LOOKED LIKE SPILT MILK
Read the book, IT LOOKED LIKE SPILT MILK, by Charles Shaw. Talk about the pictures as you read. Then take a walk outside. Lie down on the grass and look up at the clouds. Have the children find familiar creatures, shapes, people, and toys in them.
EXTENSION:
Make white felt characters to match the shapes in the book. As you read the book, put the matching shapes on the felt board. When you have finished reading the story, put additional abstract felt shapes on the felt board. Discuss what these shapes could be.

CLOUD CHART
Make a large CLOUD CHART out of posterboard. Divide the posterboard into five or six sections. In each section put a different cloud configuration — complete cover, cloudy, scattered clouds, rain clouds, no clouds, and so on. Each day the children should look outside and decide how cloudy it is and then mark the appropriate section.

ACTIVE GAMES

PARACHUTE PLAY
Bring your parachute (sheet) to circle time. Pretend that it is a quiet day and that the clouds are just sailing by. The parachute is one of the clouds and the children are the wind. As they slowly wave the sheet, let them blow with their mouths. Vary the activity by switching the hand positions as described in SCHOOL BEGINS.
EXTENSION:
Create other stories using the parachute as the main object.

140

ACTIVE GAMES

CREATIVE MOVEMENT

Have the children pretend that they are clouds moving in the sky:

- *"It's a very sunny day and you are just floating lazily through the sky. You are light and fluffy and in no hurry."*
- *"It is so windy outside. You are very dark. I think that it is going to rain. You are moving quickly across the sky in a hurry to get where you are going. I wonder if you are going to let rain fall on me?"*
- *"There are lots of clouds in the sky. You are moving along like you are dancing to fast music and each one is smiling. You must like the music."*
- *"There are hardly any clouds out today. I wonder where you are? The ones that are up there are hardly moving at all. You must be waiting for your friends or maybe you are taking a nap. You know I'm tired too. I think that I will take a nap. Good Night."* (Use again just before your rest period.)

SIMON SAYS

Simon Says,
   "Float like a cloud in the sky."
   "Twinkle like a star."
   "Supply heat like the sun."
   "Be cold like the moon."
   "Float like a cloud on a windy day."
   "Fall like a shooting star."

Remember to mix in a few statements which 'Simon' does not say. If a child does the action when s/he is not supposed to, have him/her come up and help you be 'Simon'.

BOOKS

ELPHINSTONE DAYRELL — *WHY THE SUN AND THE MOON LIVE IN THE SKY*
CHARLES SHAW — *IT LOOKED LIKE SPILT MILK*
RON WEGEN — *SKY DRAGON*

SCIENCE

AIR/WIND

FOR OPENERS

AIR IS A COLORLESS, ODORLESS GAS, BUT WE CAN SEE AND FEEL WHAT IT DOES TO THINGS. WHEN WE CAUSE AIR TO MOVE IT IS CALLED WIND.

START BY DISCUSSING THINGS WHICH ARE FAMILIAR TO THE CHILDREN. SAY,"I CAN THINK OF ONE WAY TO MAKE WIND WITH MY BODY. CAN YOU?" WHEN THEY FIGURE OUT ONE WAY, LET THEM ALL MAKE WIND. CHALLENGE THEM TO THINK OF ANOTHER WAY TO MAKE WIND WITH THEIR BODIES. THEN TRY THAT WAY.

NEXT ASK THEM TO THINK OF MACHINES IN THEIR HOMES THAT WORK US-ING AIR. WRITE THEIR IDEAS ON A LARGE SHEET OF PAPER AS THEY NAME THEM. HAVE SEVERAL OF THE SMALLER MACHINES IN A BAG. WHEN THEY THINK OF ONE YOU HAVE, TAKE IT OUT OF THE BAG. MAKE IT WORK AND THEN DISCUSS WHAT IT DOES.

HAIR DRYERS BLOW AIR OUT TO MAKE YOUR HAIR
  DRY FASTER.
VACUUM CLEANERS SUCK UP THE DIRT.
BLENDERS MIX AIR INTO DRINKS.

FINGERPLAYS

GOOD NIGHT
The little candle burns so bright,
It lights a corner of the night.
The flame is hot I'm sure you know.
To turn it off you simply blow.
Wh-h-h-h Good Night!
                Dick Wilmes

WIND TRICKS
The wind is full of tricks today,
He blew my daddy's hat away.
He chased our paper down the street.
He almost blew me off my feet.
He makes the trees and bushes dance.
Just listen to him howl and prance.

BALLOONS
This is the way we blow our balloons,
Blow, blow, blow.
This is the way we sail our balloons
Look at them go!

THE WIND
The wind came out to play one day.
He swept the clouds out of his way.
He blew the leaves and away he flew.
The trees bent low and their branches did too.
The wind blew the great big ships at sea.
And it blew my kite away from me.

RECIPES

FRESH FRUIT SHAKE

YOU'LL NEED

8 oz orange or pineapple juice
1 medium banana frozen
1 cup frozen unsweetened strawberries

TO MAKE: Combine all ingredients in a blender until smooth. The variations of this shake are limitless. Any juice or frozen fruit can be used. The banana provides the thick consistency.

From A FAMILY AFFAIR: SNACKS by Aviva Croll

WHIPPED CREAM

YOU'LL NEED

½ pint of whipping cream
1 t. honey
1 t. vanilla

TO MAKE: Whip the cream with a mixer until thick. Add the honey and vanilla while whipping. Serve with jello, pudding, or other favorites.

FIELD TRIPS

● Visit a gas station. Make arrangements with the attendant to pump up several deflated tires during your tour. Let the children explore the tires before they are inflated and then again afterwards. Are they the same? How do they feel?

LANGUAGE GAMES

SCIENCE

CREATIVE
THINKING

Read this poem to the children. As you are reading, have them close their eyes and think of the wind blowing all around them.

> *THE WIND*
> *Here we go up, up, up.*
> *Here we go down, down, down.*
> *Here we go forward.*
> *Here we go backward.*
> *Now we go 'round and 'round.*

When you have finished reading the poem, have the children name all of the things that they can think of that the wind blows around. If necessary, read the poem several times.

LANGUAGE GAMES

PUMPING AIR Bring a deflated inner tube and a hand pump to circle time. When the group is together, begin pumping up the inner tube. Let the children take turns working the pump to help you inflate the tube. As you are pumping, talk about what is happening. *"Why is the inner tube getting larger? What is going into it?"*

ECHOES Have several children stand near you. They will pretend to be the 'wind'. Say something to the children in your normal tone, such as *"Good morning, children."* As you are talking, have the 'wind' blow your message to the group. When you are finished with your message, have the group 'echo' your message back to you. Continue playing by sending other messages 'by air'. Make the messages more difficult as the children are able to remember longer sentences.

EXPLORING WIND First talk about three sources of wind again — nature, your body, and machines. *"What ways did we discover that our body could make wind? What machines worked by moving wind?"* Then wet two pieces of cloth. Hang one outside to dry in the wind. Using a hair dryer 'blow' the other one dry. *"Which one dried faster? Why?"* Smell them. *"Which one smells fresher? Why?"*

ACTIVE GAMES

BALLOONS Blow up a balloon for each child before circle time. Have them use their hands to keep it up in the air. After they have done this, have them keep it up in the air by blowing on it. Is this more difficult? Begin to play some music, let the children keep the balloons up in the air by using their hands and blowing.

ACTIVE GAMES

KITE FLYING
At art let the children make some very simple kites. Each child can cut a kite shape out of colored paper. Reinforce the bottom of the kite with clear tape. Punch a hole through the reinforced paper and then tie a three or four foot piece of string through the hole.

Each child should bring his/her kite to circle time. Go outside and let the children enjoy running with their kites trailing behind them.

EXTENSION:
- Decorate some white paper with non-toxic colored markers. Help the children fold the paper into airplanes. They can fly them around the room, to each other, or outside.
- Mobiles blow in the wind. Have the children make different parts of a mobile. Put the sections together and then let the mobile blow in the wind.

PARACHUTE PLAY
Have the children wave the parachute (sheet) in a variety of ways to create different amounts of wind. *"What ways can you move the parachute to create a lot of wind? No wind? Just a little wind?"*

GOING HOME
Make a road by putting two pieces of tape on the floor about 8" to 10" apart and about 10 feet long. Put a playhouse at the end of the road.

Give each child a ping pong ball with a face drawn on it. Let him/her try to blow his/her *'person'* down the road to home. When the child reaches home, have him/her *'welcome'* the others who are coming down the road.

S C I E N C E

BOOKS

PAT HUTCHINS — *THE WIND BLEW*
KATHERINE MARKO — *HOW THE WIND BLOWS*
CHARLOTTE ZOLOTOW — *WHEN THE WIND STOPS*

WATER

FOR OPENERS

SOME OF THE MOST COMMON SOURCES OF WATER ARE RAIN, SNOW, ICE, WELLS, LAKES, RIVERS, OCEANS, FAUCETS, AND BOTTLES. DRAW (CUT-OUT) SIMPLE PICTURES OF ALL OF THESE SOURCES. BACK EACH PICTURE WITH FELT.

DURING CIRCLE TIME, PUT THE PICTURES ON THE FELT BOARD. HAVE THE CHILDREN IDENTIFY ALL OF THE ONES THEY KNOW. TELL THEM ABOUT THE ONES WITH WHICH THEY ARE UNFAMILIAR.

EXTENSION: PUT THE PICTURES AND FELT BOARD IN THE LANGUAGE CENTER. ENCOURAGE THE CHILDREN TO TALK ABOUT THE DIFFERENT PLACES WATER IS FOUND.

FINGERPLAYS

LITTLE RAINDROPS

This is the sun, high up in the sky.
A dark cloud suddenly comes sailing by.
These are the raindrops,
Pitter, pattering down.
Watering the flowers
Growing on the ground.

JACK AND JILL

Jack and Jill went up the hill
To fetch a pail of water.
Jack fell down and broke his crown,
And Jill came tumbling after.

I'M A LITTLE TEAPOT

I'm a little teapon,
Short and stout.
Here is my handle,
Here is my spout.
When I get all steamed up,
Hear me shout,
"Just tip me over and pour me out."

I can change my handle
And my spout.
"Tip me over and pour me out."

MY BATH

I am ready for my bath tonight,
There's water in the tub.
With a piece of soap and a cloth that's wet,
My body I will rub.

I'll take the towel and dry myself.
And hurry up to bed.
You'll sing a song or lullabye
When once my prayers are said.
Dick Wilmes

RECIPES

WATER

YOU'LL NEED

Tap water
Soda water
Mineral water
Distilled water

TO MAKE: Pour the different types of water in glasses. Let the children drink the water. Discuss the differences.

WATER SNACKS

Enjoy making snacks that have a high percentage of water: jello, hot cereals, snowcones, popsicles, herb teas, etc.

FIELD TRIPS

● Visit a greenhouse in the neighborhood. Try to schedule a time when they are watering the plants. "How do they water so many plants?"

● Visit a water treatment facility. Discover where the water comes from for your area and how it is processed before you can use it.

● Call your city government and find out when they have scheduled to flush the fire hydrants near your school. Take a walk and watch them.

LANGUAGE GAMES

MAKE ICE   Make ice with the group. Put a container of water in the freezer. The next day take it out and watch it melt back into a liquid.

EVAPORATION   Introduce the word EVAPORATION. Have a child pour water in a jar. Mark a line at the water level. Put the jar on a window ledge and check it everyday. *"What is happening to the water?"* This disappearance is called *'evaporation'*.

147

LANGUAGE GAMES

CONDENSATION Boil water. (Take safety precautions.) Have the children look at the steam that is coming off of the water. Hold the lid about 8-10 inches away from the pan. When the steam hits the lid, it will liquefy. Condensation is the water formed from steam that has been cooled. Let the children watch this process. Then pass the lid around the circle for the children to see and feel the water on the lid.

RAINY, SNOWY DAYS People have different reactions to rain and snow. Ask the children, *"Do you like days when it rains? What do you like about rain? What do you do on rainy days? How about snowy days?"*

WATER, WATER EVERYWHERE Have the children name the rooms in their homes. Make a list of the rooms and then talk about the sources of water that are in each of the room. List the water sources next to the name of each room. For starters, the list will look something like:

    KITCHEN — Dish washer
                 Faucet
    BATHROOM — Faucet
                 Bathtub
                 Shower
                 Toilet
    LIVING ROOM — Condensation from plants.

EXTENSION:
Talk about the different things that water is used for. Here are a few for starters: washing, cooking, drinking, playing, caring for plants and pets, etc.

LISTEN CAREFULLY Make a tape of the different water sounds in a home. Play the tape for the children. Let them try to figure out the sources of the sounds. When the children go home, have them listen for the sounds in their house. The next day play the tape again and let the children guess again.

ACTIVE GAMES

COMING AND GOING | As the children move to and from circle time, let them pretend to be skiing, swimming, skating, and doing other water-related activities.

CHARADES | Have one child come to the front of the group. Whisper a water game such as swimming to him/her. Let the child pretend s/he is *'swimming'*. Have the remaining children try to guess what s/he is doing. Have another child pretend to do another water-related game, such as splashing, rowing a boat, skiing, fishing, etc.

CREATIVE MOVEMENT | After the group has discussed different sources of water in each room, have them pretend to be *'dish washers'*. First talk about what a *'dish washer'* does and how it gets dishes clean. *"Somebody is opening my door now and starting to load up my arms with dirty dishes. Boy, are they messy! Now they are pouring in the dish soap. Spilled some, but that doesn't matter. Close the door and turn on the switch. The water is starting to come in. Oh, it feels so warm. The soap is beginning to bubble and really tickle. I'm starting to swish the soapy water around so that I get the dishes clean. Oh, I have to rest now, that was hard work! OK, now let's rinse those dishes with nice warm water. All clean? Yes! Now I can sit awhile so that all of the dishes can dry. Oh good, someone is coming to open me up The fresh air feels so good. Somebody is taking all of the clean dishes out. I'm glad because all of those dishes were very heavy. I'm really tired and so glad that my job is finished."*

EXTENSION:

On other days, let the children pretend that they are *'washing machines'*, *'sprinklers'*, *'bathtubs'*, *'showers'*, and so on.

S
C
I
E
N
C
E

ACTIVE GAMES

SINGING

Sing this song to the tune of
LONDON BRIDGE IS FALLING DOWN

In my house there is a sink,
Is a sink, is a sink.
In my house there is a sink,
Fa la la la la.

In my house there is a washing machine,
Washing machine, washing machine.
In my house there is a washing machine,
Fa la la la la.

Add verses as the children mention different places where
they use water.

ROW, ROW, ROW YOUR BOAT

Row, row, row your boat
Gently down the stream
Merrily, merrily, merrily, merrily,
Life is but a dream.

BOOKS

FRANKLYN BRANLEY — *FLOATING AND SINKING*
PETER SPIER — *PETER SPIER'S RAIN*

COMPUTERS

FOR OPENERS

COMPUTERS ARE PART OF EVERYONE'S WORLD. CHILDREN HEAR THEIR PARENTS TALKING ABOUT USING COMPUTERS AT WORK. THEY SEE OTHERS PLAYING 'COMPUTER-CONTROLLED' VIDEO GAMES. THEY SEE PEOPLE USING COMPUTERS ON TELEVISION. THEY MAY EVEN HAVE USED ONE THEMSELVES IN SCHOOL OR AT HOME. COMPUTERS CAN BE VERY SOPHISTICATED AND HELPFUL.

TO INTRODUCE YOUR CHILDREN TO THE COMPUTER MAKE A PRETEND ONE. CONSTRUCT THE DISPLAY SCREEN FROM A LARGE HEAVY-DUTY CARDBOARD BOX WHICH YOU CAN GET FROM AN APPLIANCE OR GROCERY STORE. GET AN OLD TYPEWRITER FOR THE *KEYBOARD*. LINK THE DISPLAY SCREEN AND THE *KEYBOARD* TOGETHER WITH A PIECE OF HEAVY STRING OR ROPE.

ON THE DAY THAT YOU INTRODUCE THE 'COMPUTER' TALK ABOUT ITS COMPONENTS:

MONITOR SCREEN
KEYBOARD
PROGRAM
MEMORY

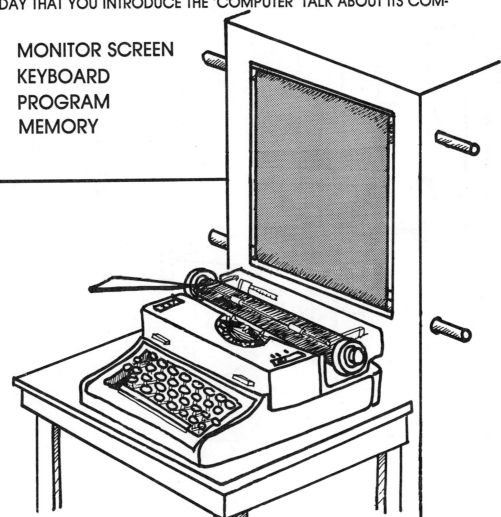

SCIENCE

151

CLASSROOM VISITOR

Have a parent who uses computers tell the children how his/her computer works, what it does, and if s/he likes working with a computer. Does it make his/her job easier? The parent can use the pretend computer to show how his/her real computer works.

LANGUAGE GAMES

NAMING YOUR COMPUTER

Once you have talked about the computer, ask the children. *"Should we give our 'computer' a name? What should we call it?"* Let the children spontaneously suggest various names. Write the names down on a large sheet of paper as the children say them. When they have all had an opportunity to suggest a name, read them all again. Then cut the names out and put them in a pail. Let one of the children pick a name out of the pail. Read the name of your classroom computer to the children. Make a sign which reads, "_____, *the Computer".* Put it near the computer.

LANGUAGE GAMES

LANGUAGE
PROGRAMS

Have several different *'programs'* for your computer. These *'programs'* should be written on separate loops which fit right into the *'monitor'*. (Use dowel rods and newspaper end-rolls or shelf paper for the loops.) Use these ideas for *'beginning programs'* and then have fun developing your own programs.

- COLOR PROGRAM: Measure the size of your *'monitor screen'*. Paint an area on the paper loop to fill the *'screen'* with one of the primary colors. Then leave some white space and paint another area with a different color. Continue leaving space between colors until you have made areas for each of the colors with which you want your children to be familiar.

- NUMBER PROGRAM: In each *'screen sized'* area on the paper loop, write a large number. Leave a blank space to separate the numbers. Make a *'screen'* for each of the numbers from 1-10. On the last *'screen'* write all of the numbers in order.

- SHAPE PROGRAM: On the first *'screen'* draw a large triangle, on the second draw a large circle, the third should be a square, and the fourth can be a rectangle. On the remaining *'screens'* draw a series of various shapes such as triangles from largest to smallest; square, circle, square, circle, _____; or square, square, rectangle, square, _____.

To use the programs with the children, bring the computer and one program to circle time. Have a child sit at the computer. Have him/her type in the name of the program you have selected to use. For example, if you have selected the SHAPE PROGRAM, have a sign that says *'SHAPE'* for the child to copy. Point to the letter *'S'* and say "S". Have the children in the circle repeat the letter "S" and the child at the computer find the *'S'* (help if needed) on the *'keyboard'* and type it in. Continue in this manner until the word *'Shape'* has been typed into the computer. When it has been *'entered'*, put the SHAPE PROGRAM on the *'monitor'*. Roll the program until the first *'Shape screen'* appears on the *'monitor'*. Ask the children, *"What shape do you see on the computer?"* Continue by going through all of the *'screens'* in your program, talking about them as you proceed.

Use other programs in a similar manner, first typing in the name and then following the directions of the program.

SCIENCE

ACTIVE GAMES

BODY
PROGRAMS

Following the construction directions under Language Games make some programs which show the children different physical activities.

• EXERCISE PROGRAM: In the first 'computer screen', draw a simple figure of a person running. In the second 'screen', show the figure touching his/her toes. For the third 'screen', draw a picture of the figure rolling. Continue by using different movements on each 'screen'.

To use this program, have a child type in the name of the program, turn it to the first 'screen', and do the exercise directed on the 'monitor'. Have a second child turn to the next 'screen' and perform the exercise. Continue.

• SCARF DANCING: On the first 'screen' draw a simple figure of a person dancing with his/her scarf high in the air. On the following 'screens', draw the figure dancing with the scarf in front, down low, over his/her shoulder, and so on.

To use the program, have a child type in the name of the program and turn the roller to the first 'screen'. Now hand out scarves and turn on dancing music. The children can begin dancing while waving their scarves high above their heads. After several minutes, turn to the next 'screen' and let the children wave their scarves according to the computer instructions.

COMMUNITY HELPERS

FOR OPENERS

COMMUNITY HELPERS SUCH AS FIREFIGHTERS, POLICE OFFICERS, LETTER CAR-
RIERS AND PARAMEDICS HAVE JOBS WHICH PROVIDE PUBLIC SERVICE TO THE
COMMUNITY. TAKE AN IMAGINARY WALK. HAVE THE CHILDREN SIT SO THEY CAN
EASILY TAP THEIR KNEES. BEGIN BY SAYING, "WE ARE GOING TO TAKE A PRETEND
WALK AROUND THE NEIGHBORHOOD. AS WE WALK, WE ARE GOING TO LOOK
AT ALL OF THE PEOPLE. LET'S START." TAP YOUR KNEES AS IF YOU ARE WALKING.
AFTER A SHORT WHILE, STOP, SAY, "I SEE A PERSON CARRYING LETTERS. HE HAS A
BIG BAG OVER HIS SHOULDER. WHO DO YOU THINK HE IS?" LET THE CHILDREN
GUESS. THEN BEGIN WALKING AGAIN. AFTER A FEW MORE STEPS, TELL A RIDDLE
ABOUT ANOTHER PERSON, MAYBE THE FIREFIGHTER WHO IS WASHING THE FIRE
TRUCK. CONTINUE THE WALK UNTIL THE CHILDREN HAVE IDENTIFIED ABOUT SIX OR
SEVEN COMMUNITY HELPERS. "IT'S BEEN A LONG WALK. LET'S GO BACK TO
SCHOOL AND HAVE A SNACK."

FINGERPLAYS

THE LIBRARIAN

The librarian helps the visitors find
Several good books to strengthen their mind.
Magazines and records are stored on a rack,
You can take some things home,
But you must bring them back.
                    Dick Wilmes

HELPFUL FRIENDS

The police officer stands so tall and straight
Holds up his hand for cars to wait.
Blows his whistle, "Tweet! Tweet!"
'Til I'm safely across the street.

Letter carriers haul a very full pack
Of letters and packages upon their back.
Step, step! Now ring, ring, ring!
Oh what surprises they will bring.

OCCUPATIONS

RECIPES

PEANUT BUTTER BALLS

Community helpers need to stay strong so they can help us when we need them. Try this energy snack.

YOU'LL NEED

½ cup of natural peanut butter
½ cup of honey
¾ to 1 cup of powdered milk

TO MAKE: Combine the honey and the peanut butter. Add the powdered milk. Shape the mixture into small balls. Roll the balls in coconut, chopped nuts or seeds.

from COME AND GET IT
by Kathleen Baxter

CLASSROOM VISITOR

● On a day that is convenient for your letter carrier, have him/her spend some time with the children explaining his/her job. Have him/her show the children his/her uniform. Explain how it changes with the seasons and that s/he has additional clothes for certain types of weather, such as a rain hat and coat for rainy weather. Let the children see how your carrier carries the mail. Other carriers carry it in a different way. How?

Once the letter carrier has left, take a walk with the children to the nearest mailbox. Talk with the children about how letters get from one place to another.

LANGUAGE GAMES

CREATIVE
THINKING

Talk about different accidents that could occur to young children, such as, *"You are riding your tricycle and you fall off as you are going around the corner. What would you do?"* Talk about other situations, how the children would react to them, and what they should do. Where they would seek assistance.

LANGUAGE GAMES

TALK ABOUT | Discuss the work that each community helper does. These discussions will be most meaningful if you have taken a recent trip to the hospital, post office, and other facilities. Have pictures to use during the talks to stimulate thinking.

- CROSSING GUARDS: *"How do guards help you? What sign do they carry? What does the sign mean?"*

- FIREFIGHTER: *"What do firefighters do? Do they wear a special uniform? What does it look like? Do they have to be strong? Why?"*

- MEDICAL PERSONNEL: *"Has a nurse ever helped you? What did s/he do for you? Who has been to see the doctor? How did the doctor help you? Who has been helped by a paramedic? What happened?"*

- POLICE: *"When have you seen police? Where were they? What were they doing?"*

- LETTER CARRIER: *"Do you ever get mail? What kind? How does your letter carrier carry the mail?"*

FIRE SAFETY | Talk about all of the things that the children must do when the fire bell rings. Show the children how to get out of the building safely. Have a fire drill.
EXTENSION:
At art have the children glue wood pieces onto paper. Then paint the wood black as if it had burned.

FELT BOARD FUN | Make all of the necessary equipment that firefighters use. Put it on the felt board. Talk about each piece.

WHAT'S MISSING? | Have a tray of postal items — stamps, letters, packages, ink pads, and so on. Have the children look at and name all of the items. Have them cover their eyes. Take away one item. Now they can open their eyes and guess which item you removed from the tray. Put the item back, have the children cover their eyes again and take another one away, and have the children guess again. Play several more times.

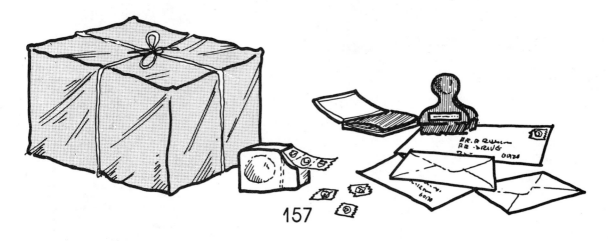

157

ACTIVE GAMES

EXERCISE
People who help us need to have strong bodies and quick brains. Begin the circle time with exercises. Let each child take a turn leading the group in his/her favorite exercise.
EXTENSION:
Letter carriers must have strong legs to carry all of the mail. Talk about exercises that would strengthen leg muscles. As you think of an exercise, do it. Start by running in place or jumping up and down.

MAIL IT
Larose m-site

Play a variation of *DUCK, DUCK, GOOSE.* Have the children sit in a circle. Have one child hold an envelope and walk around the circle saying, *"Letter"* as s/he taps each child on the head. When s/he gets to the one that s/he wants to chase her/him, have the child drop the letter and say, *"Mail it!"* Then they both run around the circle until they return to the letter. The chaser gets to *'mail'* the letter by walking around the circle and finding someone else to be the chaser.

CHARADES
The teacher should start by pretending s/he is doing an occupation. Let the children guess. If the children can, let them take turns doing an occupation for the others to guess.
EXTENSION:
Encourage the children to *'work'* in the dramatic play center during free play. Have several props available to stimulate this type of play.

BOOKS

DONNA BAKER — *I WANT TO BE A LIBRARIAN*
DONNA BAKER — *I WANT TO BE A POLICE OFFICER*
MARGARET W. BROWN — *LITTLE FIREMAN*
GENE ZION — *DEAR GARBAGE MAN*

MORE OCCUPATIONS

FOR OPENERS

CHILREN'S ORIENTATION TO WORK IS VERY LIMITED. THEY MAY BE AWARE OF THEIR PARENTS' OCCUPATIONS AND DIFFERENT JOBS THEY HAVE SEEN AS THEY GO ABOUT DAILY LIFE. CONTINUE TO BUILD ON THIS ELEMENTARY KNOWLEDGE BY FOCUSING ON OCCUPATIONS THAT THE CHILDREN CAN SEE AND WITH WHICH THEY CAN BECOME INVOLVED. TAKE A SLOW WALK AROUND THE SCHOOL'S NEIGHBORHOOD. AS YOU WALK LOOK FOR PEOPLE WHO ARE DOING A JOB. STOP AND WATCH THEM. BE AWARE OF THE TOOLS AND MACHINES THEY USE. ARE THEY WEARING A UNIFORM? WHAT SAFETY EQUIPMENT ARE THEY WEARING OR USING?

FINGERPLAYS

FRIENDS

The attendant puts gas into our car
So that we can drive it very far.
She washes our window, lifts the hood,
Checks the oil — her work is so good.

The waitress sets the table neat
At the restaurant where we eat.
She takes our order, brings our plate,
It comes so fast, we hardly wait.

The grocer stocks his shelves with care,
To make it easier shopping there.
He keeps his food so fresh and neat,
Mother says his store's a treat.

The milkman drives his truck this way.
He stops at our house 'most every day.
Brings us cool fresh milk to drink.
These are four helpful friends, I think.

DOCTOR DAY

My father said,
"It's doctor day."
Then he and I
We're on our way
To see our friend
The doctor who
Would check me out
As doctors do.

She had more things
Than I can tell

To help her keep
The people well.
She checked me up
And all the while
She wore a big
And friendly smile.

So now I hope
That someday you
May go to see
The doctor too!

OCCUPATIONS

RECIPES

MIGHTY MIXTURE

To do a job efficiently we all need to stay strong. This snack is delicious any time of the day.

YOU'LL NEED

A variety of dried fruit
  Apples
  Apricots
  Pineapple
  Raisins
A variety of seeds
  Sunflower
  Pumpkin
A variety of nuts
  Almonds
  Walnuts
  Pecans
Carob chips

TO MAKE: Mix any of the above in a large bowl. Divide in small cups and serve.

FIELD TRIPS

• It takes many types of workers to provide all of the services people need. Take a walk into the main section of your town or community. Stop at each business. Ask the children if they know what goes on in that store or building. If so, talk about what jobs the workers are doing in there. If not, tell them and then explain what the workers are doing. If arranged ahead of time and convenient, go into several of the places. Let someone show you around and explain what the people are doing.

LANGUAGE GAMES

IDENTIFYING OCCUPATIONS

Hold up pictures of people doing different kinds of work. (Magazine advertisements are a good source for pictures of telephone repair crews and operators, road construction workers, automobile mechanics, gasoline attendants, computer operators, and so on.) Have the children describe what the person is doing and what the occupation is called.

LANGUAGE GAMES

WHICH ONE DOESN'T BELONG?
Talk about all of the items that you can buy in a grocery store. Though there are 'non-food' products, most of the items are 'food-related'. After discussing food, play WHICH ONE DOESN'T BELONG? Have the children cover their eyes. Put some cans and boxes of 'food' on a tray along with one 'non-food' item. Let the children open their eyes, name everything on the tray, find which one does not belong and tell the reason why. Mix up the 'food' and put another 'non-food' item on the tray. Do this several times.

GARBAGE DAY
Have the children pretend that they are driving a garbage truck. Stop at each house and say, *"We are stopping at Josh's house.* (Use all of the children's names in your group.) *Josh, what are we picking up in your garbage today?"* Have Josh say what is going into the garbage. Continue this way until you have stopped at all of the children's homes and picked up their garbage.

CREATIVE THINKING
Play a thinking game. Have the children think about and then name all of the places in their homes where they throw or get rid of their trash. To get them started say, *"The waste basket in the bathroom."*

TALK ABOUT
Borrow different tools and supplies that a custodian uses — Push broom, scrub bucket and mop, rags, and so on. Talk about how s/he uses each tool and the supplies.

HELPING THE CUSTODIAN
Once you know what the custodian does in your school, talk about the ways that you can help him/her. Think about all of the places and items in and near the school that the custodian is responsible for keeping clean and in working condition. During the rest of the school year, help the custodian by making his/her job easier.

OCCUPATIONS

ACTIVE GAMES

MUSICAL CHAIRS Get a chair for each child. Tape a picture of a person doing a job onto each chair and put them in a circle. Have each child sit on a chair. Go around and ask each child to tell the others about the job pictured on his/her chair. Take one chair out of the circle and begin to play music. As the music is playing, have the children walk around the chairs. When the music stops, everyone should 'scramble' for a chair. The one child who does not find a seat should choose a chair, describe the job on it and remove it from the circle. Then s/he can go off to snack. Play again and again until all of the children have gone to snack.

SINGING Using the tune "OLD McDONALD HAD A FARM," teach your children "MR. GROCER HAD A STORE".

> Mr. Grocer has a store, yum, yum, yum, yum, yum.
> And in his store he had some milk, yum, yum, yum, yum, yum.
> With a gulp-gulp here and a gulp-gulp there
> Here a gulp, there a gulp, everywhere a gulp-gulp.
> Mr. Grocer had a store, yum, yum, yum, yum, yum.

Continue:
APPLES — Crunch, crunch, crunch
POPCORN — Pop, pop, pop
CARROTS — Munch, munch, munch

BOOKS

CHILDREN'S PRESS —*I WANT TO BE. . .(series)*
ANNE ROCKWELL — *WHEN WE GROW UP*
WENDY SAUL —*BUTCHER, BAKER, CABINETMAKER: Photographs of Women at Work*

162

TOOLS

FOR OPENERS

BEGIN SEVERAL CIRCLE TIMES BY IDENTIFYING DIFFERENT CATEGORIES OF TOOLS — HOUSEHOLD, YARD, AND WORKBENCH. INTRODUCE EACH CATEGORY OF TOOLS BY HAVING A TRAY FULL OF THAT TYPE.

HOUSEHOLD SCISSORS, EGG BEATER, CAN OPENER, ROLLING PIN, WISK BROOM, ETC. HOLD UP EACH TOOL. IF A CHILD KNOWS THE NAME OF THE TOOL, HAVE HIM / HER PRETEND TO BE USING IT. CALL ON A CHILD TO SAY THE NAME ALOUD.

YARD HOE, SHOVEL, PAIL, MODEL (TOY) WHEELBARROW, WEEDER, CLIPPERS, LAWN SEEDER, AND SO ON. FIRST HAVE THE CHILDREN IDENTIFY THE NAME OF EACH TOOL. THEN PLAY "WHAT'S MISSING". HAVE THE CHILDREN COVER THEIR EYES. TAKE ONE OF THE TOOLS AWAY. HAVE THEM UNCOVER THEIR EYES AND NAME THE TOOL THAT IS MISSING. PUT THE TOOL BACK AND PLAY AGAIN.

WORKBENCH HAMMER, DRILL, SCREWDRIVER, WRENCH, PLIERS, VISE, AND SO ON. HOLD UP EACH TOOL. HAVE THE CHILDREN WHO KNOW THE NAME STAND UP. HAVE THEM SAY THE NAME ALOUD AND SIT BACK DOWN. HOLD UP ANOTHER TOOL AND IDENTIFY IT IN THE SAME WAY. CONTINUE UNTIL ALL OF THE TOOLS HAVE BEEN NAMED.

FINGERPLAYS

HAMMER AND SAW

"Pound, pound, pound"
Says the little hammer.
Pound, pound, pound,
Pound the nails in tight.
"Saw, saw, saw"
Says the little saw.
Saw, saw, saw,
Saw the board just right.

FINGERPLAYS

TOOLS

If you spilled flour all over the floor,
Or found dust and leaves right next to the door,
You wouldn't use a hammer to clean up the room,
You'd reach for your dust pan and probably a _____.

While painting, your sister got green on the table.
You want to clean it, I know you are able.
You won't use an axe, a ladder, or nail,
You'll reach for some water, a rag, and a _____.

You're helping your mother who is fixing the fence,
But you missed with the hammer and now there are dents.
To smooth out the lumber and finish the caper,
Don't use a pipe wrench instead of sand _____.

Dick Wilmes

HELPING THE FAMILY

I help my family by
Sweeping the floor,
Dusting the table, and
Polishing the door.
Beating the eggs,
Sifting the flour, and
Pounding the pegs.
'Til my bedtime hour.

RECIPES

CHEESE HAMMERS

YOU'LL NEED

Cheese chunks
Pretzel sticks

TO MAKE: Cut a variety of cheeses in small squares. Poke a pretzel into each one. Just before you eat your "hammer" say the fingerplay 'Hammer and Saw.'

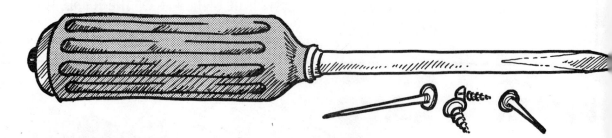

CLASSROOM VISITOR

● Ask one of the parents who is a carpenter or who does a lot of building as a hobby to visit your class. Ask him/her to bring several tools, some screws, and nails so that s/he can demonstrate how the tools are used. If s/he can spend a morning or afternoon in the class, ask him/her to build a simple stool or other piece with the children. If the parent would prefer, s/he might fix any of the wooden toys that have broken.

LANGUAGE GAMES

CATEGORIZING TOOLS

Have a tray full of household, yard, and workbench tools. Hold up the tools one at a time. Have the group whisper which category that tool belongs in. As the children say the category, put the tool into an appropriate pile.
EXTENSION:
Put the household tools in the housekeeping center and the workbench tools on the workbench. (Remember safety rules!)

FEEL AND GUESS

At art have each child decorate a paper bag. At circle time give each child his/her bag with a tool in it. They should not look into the bag. After everyone has a bag, have the children put their hand into the bag and feel around the entire tool. When a child thinks s/he knows what it is, have him/her stand up. When everyone is standing, go around the circle and let each child say the name of the tool, then take it out and see if the guess was correct.

RIDDLES

Have a variety of tools displayed in the middle of the circle. Describe how one of the tools works. Let the children guess which tool you are talking about. For example say, *"This tool can be held in your hand, is long, and has lots of sharp points. What is it?"* Continue by describing all of the tools.
VARIATION:
Instead of describing how the tool looks, describe its function. For example, *"A person's arm moves this tool back and forth. As it moves, it cuts wood. What is it?"*

TALK ABOUT

Talk about the experiences that the children have had using different tools while helping their family and friends. Start with a question such as, *"Who helps their mom and dad in the kitchen?"* Let the children tell about the tools they use as they relate their kitchen experiences. Continue the discussion by talking about outside activities and woodworking projects.

OCCUPATIONS

165

LANGUAGE GAMES

IDENTIFYING TOOLS

Children will be able to readily identify some tools and others will be more difficult, and still others will be totally unfamiliar to them. Play several games to help children become more familiar with the names of different tools and their functions.

- Have seven or eight tools you think your children can name. Hold them up one at a time. Let a child name a tool and then come up and demonstrate how it is used.
- Have several slightly unfamiliar tools. Hold them up one at a time and see if any of the children can name them and show how they are used. If not, introduce the new tools and their function to the children.
- Give each child a tool. One at a time have each child stand and hold up his/her tool. Have someone in the group name the tool. Have someone else demonstrate it.

ACTIVE GAMES

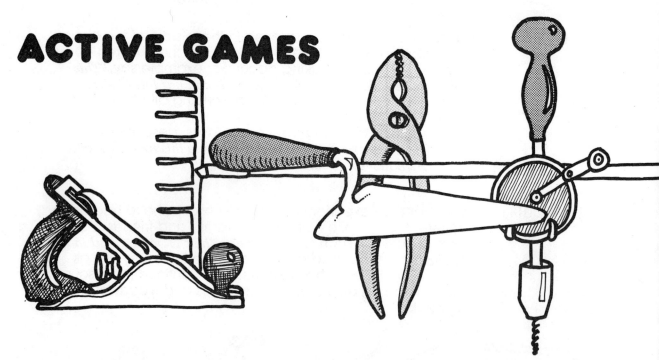

CHARADES

Have a group of tools in the middle of the circle. The teacher (or child) pretends to be using one of the tools. The children guess which tool it is. Have one child go to the middle and hold up that tool. Continue.

MOVING

Have the children stand up. The teacher holds up one of the tools, such as a shovel. Let the children pretend that they are using the shovel. As the children are using the shovel, chant, *"We are digging, digging, digging all day long."* Hold up another tool such as a rake. Let the children pretend they are raking. Chant, *"We are raking, raking, raking all day long."*

ACTIVE GAMES

SINGING   Teach the children the chant, *JOHNNY WORKS WITH ONE HAMMER.*

> *Johnny works with one hammer, one hammer, one hammer.*
> *Johnny works with one hammer,* (Pound with one fist.)
> *Now he works with two.*

> *Johnny works with two hammers, two hammers, two hammers.*
> *Johnny works with two hammers,* (Pound with two fists.)
> *Now he works with three.*

> *Johnny works with three hammers. . .* (Pound with two fists
> & one foot.)

> *Johnny works with four hammers. . .* (Pound with two fists
> & two feet.)

> *Johnny works with five hammers, five hammers, five hammers.*
> *Johnny works with five hammers,* (Pound with two fists,
> two feet & one head.)
> *Now he goes to sleep.* (Lay down.)

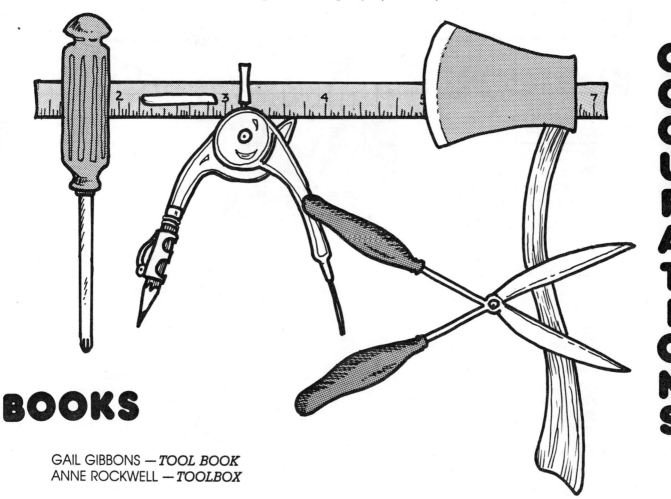

BOOKS

GAIL GIBBONS — *TOOL BOOK*
ANNE ROCKWELL — *TOOLBOX*

OCCUPATIONS

MACHINES

FOR OPENERS

GATHER AS MANY TOY OR MODEL PIECES OF MACHINERY AS YOU CAN. GET SOME THAT ARE USED IN THE HOME, ON THE FARM, AND FOR ROAD REPAIR. HAVE ALL OF THE MACHINERY IN A GROUP IN FRONT OF YOU. HAVE THE CHILDREN LOOK CLOSELY AT THE DIFFERENT PIECES YOU HAVE. DISCUSS THE THINGS THAT ARE SIMILAR ABOUT ALL OF THE MACHINES. THEN FIND THINGS THAT ARE DIFFERENT. NEXT ASK THE CHILDREN, "WHICH OF THESE MACHINES DO YOU THINK YOU COULD USE IN YOUR HOME?" "ON THE FARM?" "TO REPAIR ROADS?" SEPARATE THEM INTO PILES.

EXTENSION: PUT THE MACHINERY IN THE BLOCK AREA. ENCOURAGE THE CHILDREN TO BUILD STRUCTURES THAT RELATE TO THE TYPES OF MACHINERY THEY ARE USING, SUCH AS BARNS FOR THE TRACTORS AND WAGONS.

FINGERPLAYS

FARM CHORES

Five little farmers
Woke up with the sun.
It was early morning
And the chores must be done.

The first little farmer
Went out to milk the cow.
The second little farmer
Thought he'd better plow.

The third little farmer
Cultivated weeds.
The fourth little farmer
Planted more seeds.

The fifth little farmer
Drove his tractor 'round.
Five little farmers
The best that can be found.
(Talk about the machines that
the farmers used to do their chores.)

THE STEAMSHOVEL

The steamshovel scoop opens its mouth
  soooooooooooo wide;
Then scoops up the dirt and lays it aside.

YOUR WASHING MACHINE

You can take your dirty clothes
And throw them in a tub,
Grab a bar of soap and board
And scrub, and scrub, and scrub.
    OR
Learn to use the washing machine
At the laundromat.
It'll clean your clothes in half the time,
What do you think of that?
          Dick Wilmes

RECIPES

VENDING MACHINE SNACKS
YOU'LL NEED

Using a large appliance box, construct a vending machine. Use the machine to distribute the snacks to the children each day. At snack time give each child a piece of play money. Have him/her insert the coin into the machine. A ''hidden person'' will then *vend* the snack to the child.

Peanuts
Raisins
Fresh Fruit
Sunflower seeds
Pretzels

FIELD TRIPS

● Send a request home to your parents asking if anyone is planning to put in a new driveway, sidewalk, or patio. Ask them to let you know when the cement truck will be there. At that time walk over to the home and watch the cement truck and the workers pour the cement. (Take safety precautions.)

● Call a local tree trimming company and see if they are going to be working in your neighborhood. When they are working watch them. Talk about the different types of machinery they use. Please be safe. You'll need to stand back.

● Are the roads being repaired in your area? Watch the workers patch the holes, construct new roads, and so on. What do you call the different pieces of machinery that they use?

LANGUAGE GAMES

SPINNER FUN

Make a spinner game to help the children learn the names of different pieces of farm machinery. Cut a large circle (about 18'' in diameter) out of poster board. Divide it into eight or more equal sections. Glue a picture of a farm machine in each section. Make a spinner and attach it to the center of the circle with a brad.

At circle time, have a child come up and flick the spinner. When it stops, ask the children to call out the name of the machine that the spinner is pointing to. How is that piece of machinery used?

LANGUAGE GAMES

CREATIVE
THINKING
Machines and tools help people work and play. Ask the children to think of all of the machines they or their parents use around the house. As they name a machine, list it on a chart and discuss how it is used.

NAME THE
MACHINE
After the children know the names of the major pieces of road building machinery, tell them a simple story about road construction. As you tell the story, leave out the names of the machinery. The children should try to identify the pieces of equipment as you tell the story. *"Everyday before school Peter and Alice* (Use the names of two of the children in your class.)*watched the construction workers building a new road near their home. They stood far enough away so that they would be safe. In the beginning several men broke up the old road using a* (jack hammer)*. When the old concrete was in big chunks, it was lifted by a* (front-end loader)*into big* (dump trucks)*. The workers in the trucks took the old concrete away. Then a construction crew leveled out the dirt that was under the old road. When everything was ready, other workers came and poured new concrete for the road from large* (cement trucks)*. Once the concrete was poured, workers smoothed it out. Everyone stayed off the road until it was completely dry. Workers from the city came and made the white lines down the middle of the road. After many days it was finally ready for everyone to use. That evening when our family was together, we all got into our car and took a drive on the new road.*

FELT BOARD FUN
Before circle time look through a *'home and garden'* magazine to find pictures of lawnmowers, hedge clippers, and other types of machinery. Cut them out and back them with felt. On the first day you are talking about home machinery, put these pictures on the felt board. Ask the children if they know what the machine is called and how it is used. Continue this discussion using all of the pictures that you have found.

ACTIVE GAMES

WALK IN CONCRETE

As an art activity before circle time, make hand or foot prints of each child in plaster of paris. Then at circle time talk about how the plaster felt. Tell the children that the plaster is similar to the concrete used to build roads, driveways, sidewalks, and so on. Relate the discussion to your recent field trip to a child's home or to watch a new road being built. Now have the children think about what it would feel like to walk in wet concrete. Walk around the room pretending that the floor is made of *wet concrete* and that you are walking in it up to your ankles. Now pretend that you are walking in *wet concrete* up to your knees.

FOLLOW THE LEADER

Follow the leader around the room. The leader operates different pieces of machinery. When you change the piece of machinery, call out its name.
* CRANE — Crank the bucket up and down.
* JACK HAMMER — Vibrate as if you were breaking concrete.
* WASHING MACHINE — Twist back and forth.
* CLOTHES DRYER — Flop around and blow out.
* TRACTOR — Pretend to be steering.
* COMBINE — Roll your arms around.

VARIATION:
Take turns with the children pretending that you are working one of the machines. Let the others guess what machine it is.

ACTIVE GAMES

SINGING

• Sing this song to the tune of *FARMER IN THE DELL.*
Talk with the children about the pieces of machinery needed to do each function.

The farmer in the dell,
The farmer in the dell,
Hi, ho, the dairy-o,
The farmer in the dell.

The farmer plows his land,
The farmer plows his land,
Hi, ho, the dairy-o,
The farmer plows his land.

The farmer plants his seed,

The farmer weeds his fields,

The farmer waters his crops,

The farmer watches them grow,

The farmer harvests his crops,

• Sing this song to the tune of *LONDON BRIDGE IS FALLING DOWN.* As you're singing, do the appropriate actions.

Cut the hay and bundle it up,
Bundle it up, bundle it up.
Cut the hay and bundle it up,
Oh, good farmer.

Take the hay and put it on the wagon,
Put it on the wagon, put it on the wagon.
Take the hay and put it on the wagon,
Oh, good farmer.

Drive the hay into the barn,
Into the barn, into the barn.
Drive the hay into the barn,
Oh, good farmer.

Feed the horses with the hay,
With the hay, with the hay.
Feed the horses with the hay,
Oh, good farmer.

BOOKS

TANA HOGAN — *DIG, DRILL, DUMP, FILL*
ANNE ROCKWELL — *MACHINES*
GEORGE ZAFFO — *AIRPLANES & TRUCKS & TRAINS, FIRE ENGINES & BOATS & SHIPS, & BUILDING & WRECKING MACHINES*

BRUSHES

FOR OPENERS

THERE ARE MANY TYPES OF BRUSHES — PAINT BRUSHES, SCRUB AND OTHER HOUSEHOLD BRUSHES, MAKE-UP BRUSHES, TOOTH, HAIR, AND OTHER ASSORTED BODY CARE BRUSHES, CLOTHES BRUSHES, AND SO ON. HAVE A 'BRUSH HUNT'. BEFORE CIRCLE TIME, HIDE A VARIETY OF BRUSHES AROUND THE ROOM.

AT CIRCLE TIME, GIVE EACH CHILD A BAG. WHEN YOU BEGIN THE MUSIC, LET THE CHILDREN START LOOKING FOR THE BRUSHES HIDDEN IN THE ROOM. WHEN THE MUSIC STOPS, HAVE THEM COME BACK TO THE CIRCLE AND TAKE THE BRUSHES THEY FOUND OUT OF THEIR BAGS. LET EACH CHILD HOLD UP A BRUSH AND LET THE OTHERS CALL OUT WHAT KIND OF BRUSH IT IS. IF ANY OF THE CHILDREN HAVE EVER USED THAT TYPE OF BRUSH, ENCOURAGE HIM / HER TO TELL ABOUT IT.

FINGERPLAYS

BRUSHES IN MY HOME

The brushes in my home
Are simply everywhere.
I use them for my teeth each day,
And also for my hair.

We use them in the kitchen sink
And in the toilet bowls.
For putting polish on my shoes,
And to waterproof the soles.

Brushes are used to polish the floors,
And also paint the wall,
To clean the charcoal barbecue,
It's hard to name them all.
                    Dick Wilmes

SHINY SHOES

First I loosen mud and dirt,
My shoes I then rub clean.
For shoes in such a dreadful sight
Never should be seen.

I spread the polish on the shoes,
And then I let it dry.
I brush the shoes until they shine
And sparkle in my eye.

OCCUPATIONS

RECIPES

- Let the children scrub raw vegetables with vegetable brushes.
- Make different kinds of rolls. Glaze them with one of these toppings. Use a pastry brush.

  EGG WHITE GLAZE

  YOU'LL NEED

  2 egg whites
  1 t. cold water

  TO MAKE: Put the egg whites in a small bowl. Add 1 t. of water and beat together.

  EGG YELLOW GLAZE

  YOU'LL NEED

  Several egg yolks
  A drop or two of water

  TO MAKE: Put egg yolks in a small bowl. Beat them until they are broken up. Add a drop or two of water if needed.

FIELD TRIPS

- Call the city garage and make arrangements for the class to see the street sweeper. Have the attendant show the children all of the features, but especially the giant brushes. If safe, let the children get close enough to touch the brushes and see how large they really are.

CLASSROOM VISITOR

- Have the custodian bring the floor polisher into the class and show the children how it operates. If s/he has some additional time, s/he might be able to polish one small section of the floor or hallway. The children can then see how shiny the brush gets the floor. Over the next several days watch that section of the floor and see what happens to it.

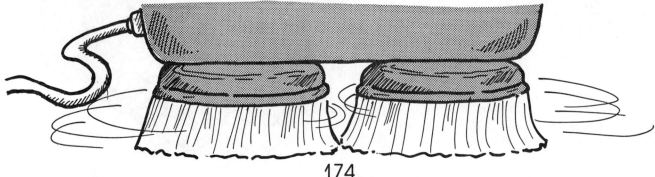

LANGUAGE GAMES

TALK ABOUT
Each day talk about a different type of brush. Have a variety of brushes which are included in the category which you are discussing, such as different household brushes. Talk about their shapes and use. Pass each brush around and let the children feel it. Let the children pretend to use each brush.
EXTENSION:
Put several different brushes at the easel each day.

RIDDLES
Describe a brush and its purpose. Let the children guess which brush you are talking about. For example, *"I have a very long handle. I am used mostly in the kitchen. I help clean the floors. What am I?"*
EXTENSION:
Let the children make up the riddles. This is often difficult for young children, so they may need help.

BRUSHES HELP WORKERS
Take every opportunity to relate brushes to different occupations. For example, talk about how the dentist uses brushes. *"Is the dentist's brush like the toothbrush that you use at home? Does it make noise? Why? Does yours? How does it feel?"* Continue by discussing painters, artists, garage attendants, and so forth.

FEEL AND GUESS
Put all types of brushes in a bag. Let a child reach in and pick one. Before s/he pulls it out let him/her guess what kind of brush it is.
VARIATION:
Let the children reach in and describe the brush he is feeling to the other children. Let the group guess what kind of brush it might be.

BRUSH MATCH
Get a large piece of board, pictures of people using brushes (from magazines and newspapers), and the matching real brushes. Glue the pictures on the posterboard and cover with clear adhesive. Put the brushes in a box and the board into the middle of the circle. Hold up one brush at a time and have the children name it and then match it to one of the pictures.

OCCUPATIONS

ACTIVE GAMES

PASS THE BRUSH
Bring several brushes to circle time. Pick one, name it and its uses, and begin passing it to music. Stop the music and see who is holding the brush. Say, *"Ryan is holding the brush."* Have the child put the brush in the middle of the circle and select a different brush. Start again. Play until all of the brushes are in the center of the circle.

MOVING
Have the children pretend that their feet are brushes. Play some music and have them begin to move. As the children are moving, walk around and ask them what type of brush their feet are pretending to be. Have the children play this another time pretending that their hands are the brushes.

CURLING
Introduce the game of CURLING to your group. It is a game which is played with brooms and very smooth heavy stones on ice. In curling, one player slides the heavy stone along the ice toward a target at the other end of the rink. Two of his team mates use brooms and sweep the ice in front of the stone which helps the stone slide faster.

Vary the game so that your children can enjoy it on the playground. Let them use balls and small brooms. They can enjoy swishing the brooms around trying to move the balls. You might want to make a line with tape or chalk and let them brush the ball across the line. Children can enjoy playing by themselves or passing the ball to each other.

SINGING
Teach your children new words to the tune:*"HERE WE GO 'ROUND THE MULBERRY BUSH."*

> *This is the way we sweep the floor,*
> *Sweep the floor, sweep the floor.*
> *This is the way we sweep the floor,*
> *All on a Monday morning.*
>
> *This is the way we brush our teeth.*
>
> *This is the way we brush our hair.*
>
> *This is the way we polish our nails.*
>
> *This is the way we scrub the floor.*
>
> *This is the way we shine our shoes.*

BOOKS

AUGUSTA GOLDIN —*STRAIGHT HAIR, CURLY HAIR*
ETHYL & LEONARD KESSLER —*OUR TOOTH STORY; A TALE OF TWENTY TEETH*
HARLOW ROCKWELL —*MY DENTIST*
PETER SPIER —*OH! WERE THEY EVER HAPPY*

BUILDINGS

FOR OPENERS

FIND PICTURES OF ALL TYPES OF BUILDINGS:

DWELLING

HOSPITAL

FIRE STATION

FACTORY

BARN

ANY OTHERS

GLUE EACH PICTURE TO A PIECE OF CONSTRUCTION PAPER. HOLD UP ONE PICTURE AT A TIME. HAVE THE CHILDREN IDENTIFY WHAT TYPE OF BUILDING IT IS. ALSO ASK, "HOW DO YOU KNOW IT IS A _____?" LET THE CHILDREN TRY TO TELL HOW THEY RECOGNIZE THIS KIND OF BUILDING. HELP THE CHILDREN BE SPECIFIC. CONTINUE THE DISCUSSION BY ASKING, "WHAT DO YOU THINK PEOPLE DO INSIDE THIS BUILDING?"

FINGERPLAYS

THE FIRE STATION

The fire station's empty,
There's no-one there today.
Do you think they're on vacation
Or just gone out to play?
        "NOOOOOO"

The big red doors are open
The fire trucks aren't there.
The ambulance is leaving now,
Their sirens fill the air.

I know they're at a fire.
I saw the trucks go past,
With sirens screaming loudly,
Their red and blue lights flashed.

They're racing to the Miller Barn,
There's a fire in the hay,
They'll use their water hoses,
And then they'll drive away.
                Dick Wilmes

MY HOUSE

I'm going to build a little house,
With windows big and bright.
With chimney tall and curling smoke,
Drifting out of sight.

In winter when the snowflakes fall,
Or when I hear a storm,
I'll go sit in my little house,
Where I'll be snug and warm.

THE FACTORY

The whistle blows at the factory
To signal the start of the machinery.
The workers are busy from morning 'til lunch,
When they can sit down and eat in a bunch.
At the end of the day the whistle will blow,
The machinery will stop and the workers will go.
                Dick Wilmes

OCCUPATIONS

RECIPES

FINGER SANDWICHES

Make some fancy finger sandwiches for your restaurant.

YOU'LL NEED

A variety of breads
Cream cheese
Toppings such as:
  Apple slices
  Dates
  Walnuts
  Olives
  Pimentos
  Raisins

TO MAKE: Cut the breads into different shapes. Spread the cheese on each piece of bread. Top with any of the garnishes.

FIELD TRIPS

● Take a walk through your town and simply note all of the buildings: the bakery, gas station, dime store, laundry, office buildings, and so on. Ask someone from the local historical society to come and tell the children what the town used to look like. If the person has some pictures or models of the main street or section, have him/her bring them to show the children. When the visitor is telling the children about how the town used to look, s/he will have to be very specific about what new building replaced which old building. For example, s/he will need to say, "You know where the fire station is. Before the fire station was there, Mr. Jones had his bakery in that spot."

LANGUAGE GAMES

CREATIVE THINKING

Talk about how you can recognize what a building is used for. For example, hold up a picture of a firehouse. *"How do you know this is a firehouse?"* Do this with several more familiar buildings such as a barn, automobile garage, etc.
EXTENSION:
Find pictures of unusual buildings. Hold them up one at a time and talk about what kind of building it might be. Even if you know the specific purpose, let the children figure out all of the possibilities.

LANGUAGE GAMES

FLIP BOOK

Make a *'Flip Book'* about buildings and the people who work in them.

YOU'LL NEED
- Sturdy cardboard
- Metal rings
- Pictures of buildings

TO MAKE: Cut one piece of cardboard 6" x 8". to use as the back of the *'Flip Book'.* Make two sets of cards, each 6" x 4". Assemble the *'Flip Book'* by punching a hole through both sets of cards and attaching one set to the top and the other set to the bottom of the back of the *'Flip Book'* using metal clip rings. Find pictures of people and associated buildings that the children can match. For example, a firefighter and fire station, a nurse and hospital, a letter carrier and post office, and so on. Paste the people on the top set of cards and the buildings on the bottom set. Mix the cards up so that you must *'flip'* the pages to find a pair.

Hold the book up, have the children identify the person. Then begin flipping the building pictures. When you get to the building that matches the person, have the children say, *"Stop!"* Discuss the match. Go to the next picture and match that person with the correct building. Play until all of the people and buildings have been matched.

OCCUPATIONS

LANGUAGE GAMES

TALK ABOUT
Ask the children, *"Have any of you ever been to a gas station?"* The answer will probably be *"Yes!"* Then ask, *"Who did you go with? What did you do there?"* Talk about what the child did at the gas station. After each child describes what happened at the gas station, ask the others if they had similar experiences.

EXTENSION:
People work in other types of buildings besides gas stations. Let the children think about where their moms and dads work. Let each say where his/her parent/s work. Tape record what each child says. Play the tape back. See if any of the children can recognize who is talking.

RESTAURANTS
Say to the children, *"You are really going to have to put on your thinking caps.* (Pretend to put them on.) *Think about all of the buildings that you have been in which serve food."* Have a large sheet of paper. As the children say a place where they have been, write it on the paper. After they have thought about all of the places, read the list. Is there any one place or maybe several where all of the children have been?

EXTENSION:
Cut out a variety of pictures of popular foods. Back them with felt and put them on the felt board. Using the restaurant list that you just made, talk about the foods that you would eat in each place. Say, *"If you were going to eat at Burger Town, what would you have?"* Continue asking about 4 or 5 of the places on the list. When the children answer, point to the foods that they say.

ACTIVE GAMES

OBSTACLE COURSE
Set up an obstacle course inside. Along the course have large boxes that you have made into different types of *'buildings'*. As the children pass each *'building'*, have them tell you what type of *'building'* it is.*

ACTIVE GAMES

WALK THROUGH THE TOWN
Make a 'sidewalk' out of tape. Using the buildings that you made for the obstacle course, build the business district of your town along the 'sidewalk'. Staying on the line, walk down to the post office, grocery store, etc. Stop at each building and talk about what is going on inside of it.

CREATIVE MOVEMENT
Let each child be an 'airplane'. Decide where you are going to fly. Talk about the 'airport'. Pretend that you are on the 'runway' and the 'controllers' have given you permission to 'take-off'. "Our wings are level and we taxi onto the runway. Now we are ready for takeoff. Going slowly at first, we gain speed to take-off. Up, up, up we go! Flying through the sky, we begin to climb higher until we can see far into the distance and the cars below us look very small. First we fly straight with our wings level. Now we tilt our wings to the side so that we will turn . Finally we reach our destination and ask the controller to give us permission to land our plane. Our wheels are touching the ground now and we slow down and taxi to the terminal. All of the passengers are getting off now and the airport workers are getting the luggage out of the cargo area. Time to taxi to our hanger and rest until the next flight."

SINGING
• Play IN AND OUT THE WINDOW. Have all of the children form a circle and hold hands. While holding hands, have them raise their arms up to form 'windows'. Let each child have a turn weaving 'in and out the windows'. Chant as you play.

> Alicia goes in and out the windows,
> In and out the windows,
> In and out the windows.
> Alicia goes in and out the windows,
> As we did before.

Change name while each child goes weaving in and out under the arms of the children.

• Sing this song to the tune of "HERE WE GO 'ROUND THE MULBERRY BUSH".

> This is the way we pump the gas,
> Pump the gas, pump the gas,
> This is the way we pump the gas,
> Right into your car.

Continue with other verses using the parents' jobs.

BOOKS

BYRON BARTON — *BUILDING A HOUSE*
ANNE ROCKWELL — *MACHINES*
GEORGE ZAFFO — *AIRPLANES & TRUCKS & TRAINS, FIRE ENGINES & BOATS & SHIPS, & BUILDING & WRECKING MACHINES*

OCCUPATIONS

TOYS

FOR OPENERS

GET A VARIETY OF TOYS FROM YOUR CLASSROOM. HAVE SEVERAL THAT OPERATE BY SPRINGS, SOME THAT ARE STUFFED, OTHERS THAT ARE USED FOR BUILDING, A COUPLE OF RHYTHM INSTRUMENTS, AND A FEW WHEELED TOYS. PUT THE TOYS IN FRONT OF YOU. HAVE THE CHILDREN LOOK AT THE PILE FROM WHERE THEY ARE SITTING. LET EACH CHILD COME UP, GET A TOY, AND THEN SIT DOWN. DO THIS UNTIL EACH CHILD HAS AT LEAST ONE TOY. NOW HAVE THE CHILDREN LOOK AT THEIR TOY. SAY TO THEM, " IF YOU HAVE A STUFFED TOY, PLEASE BRING IT BACK TO ME." HAVE THEM PUT THE STUFFED TOYS IN A PILE. CONTINUE IN THIS MANNER UNTIL ALL THE TOYS ARE RETURNED AND SORTED.

FINGERPLAYS

TEDDY BEAR
Teddy bear, teddy bear,
Turn around.
Teddy bear, teddy bear,
Touch the ground.

Teddy bear, teddy bear,
Show your shoe.
Teddy bear, teddy bear,
That will do.

Teddy bear, teddy bear,
Go upstairs.
Teddy bear, teddy bear,
Say your prayers.

Teddy bear, teddy bear,
Turn out the light.
Teddy bear, teddy bear,
Say, "Good night".

FLOPSY FLORA
I'm just like Flopsy Flora,
My doll that's made of rags.
My arms go flop — my feet go plop,
My head just wigs and wags.

JACK-IN-THE-BOX
Jack-in-the-box,
Jack-in-the-box,
Won't you come out?
Yes, I will!!

HERE'S A BALL
Here's a ball,
And here's a ball,
And a great big ball, I see.
Shall we count them?
Are you ready?
ONE! TWO! THREE!

RECIPES

Make a variety of eatable balls

CHEESE BALLS

YOU'LL NEED

8 oz cream cheese, softened
1 stick of butter, softened
2 cups grated cheddar cheese
½ package of onion soup mix

TO MAKE: Blend all of the ingredients well. Shape into small balls. Roll in chopped nuts if desired.

CRUNCHY CARROT BALLS

YOU'LL NEED

3 oz cream cheese, softened
½ cup shredded cheddar cheese
1 t. honey
1 cup finely shredded carrots
½ cup Grape Nuts cereal

TO MAKE: In a medium mixing bowl, beat the cream cheese, cheddar cheese, and honey together until well blended. Stir in shredded carrots. Cover and chill for about 30 minutes. Shape into balls, cover and chill. Just before serving, roll the balls in the cereal.

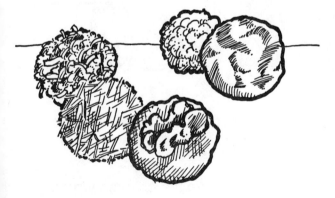

YUMMY BALLS

YOU'LL NEED

½ cup peanut butter
½ cup honey
½ cup cocoa/carob powder
1 cup toasted wheat germ
1 cup chopped peanuts
½ cup sunflower seeds

TO MAKE: Combine all of the above ingredients and roll into balls. Roll the balls in coconut.

CEREAL BALLS

YOU'LL NEED

1 cup 'ground-in-a-blender' cereal, such as shredded wheat, granola, wheat germ, etc.
1 T. honey
1 T. peanut butter (optional)
Milk as needed

TO MAKE: After grinding the cereal in a blender, add honey, peanut butter, and blend. Add as much milk as necessary so that the mixture can be rolled into balls. Refigerate in a covered container.

"CANDY" BALLS

YOU'LL NEED

1 cup natural peanut butter
¼ cup carob powder
½ cup mashed bananas
2 t. vanilla

TO MAKE: Mix all of the ingredients together. Shape into balls and roll in cinnamon. If desired, press a walnut half on each ball. Store in the refrigerator.

FIELD TRIPS

- Take a Stuffed Toy Walk. In conjunction with other activities on Stuffed Toy Day, take the toys for a walk around the block. As you are walking, look for "real" people, animals, or things like the stuffed toys. For example the child who brings a stuffed dog or cat would look for a real dog or cat. A child who brings a doll, would look for a real person, and so on.

RECREATION

LANGUAGE GAMES

STUFFED TOY DAY

Have a *'Stuffed Toy Day'*. Encourage every child to bring a special stuffed toy to school on a pre-arranged day. (Have several extra stuffed toys for children who have left theirs at home.)
- Have each child bring the toy to circle time. Go around the group and have each child tell what type of toy s/he brought. Go around again and let each child have a chance to tell his/her toy's name.
- Give those children who want, an opportunity to tell a story, joke, or a favorite thing about their stuffed friend.
- Play *'I See A Stuffed Toy'*. Have each child put the toy in front of him/herself so that everybody can see each other's toy. Describe one of the toys. The children should look around trying to figure out which toy you are talking about. When they know, have them point to it. If that's the one, have the child with that toy hold it up. If the correct toy was not identified, continue your description until one of the children has figured it out. Continue by describing each of the children's stuffed toys.

WHEEL TOYS

Before circle time, gather a variety of toys that have wheels. Talk about the sizes of the wheels. *"Why are there different sizes? Are the wheels all the same color?"*
EXTENSION:
- Build a ramp with large blocks. Have the children watch closely as you let several toys go down the ramp.
  "Which one went fastest?"
  "Which one went farthest?"
  "Did any turn as they came off the ramp? Which one? Why? Which way?"
  "Which ones went straight?"
- Mix and match the other toys and have several more races.
- At art do printing with cars and trucks. Dip the wheels into paint and *'drive'* them along white paper.

LANGUAGE GAMES

LOOK FOR
SHAPES

Gather several toys in the room that have various shapes in them. Let the children examine the toys and then discuss what shapes are in the toy. For example, a car has square windows, round headlights, rectangular doors, etc.

ACTIVE GAMES

MOVING

Move around the circle like different toys. Have as many actual toys as you can, so that the children see each toy moving and then can more easily pretend to be that toy.
- Boing like springs in the Jack-in-the-Box.
- Wind-up like dolls and race cars.
- Roll like balls or roller skates.
- Walk like mechanical toys.
- Skate like a pair of ice or roller skates.
- Glide like a skateboard.

HULA HOOP
FUN

Get several large 'hula hoops'. Have the children:
- Jump in and out of the hoop.
- Jump, skip, hop, walk, and so on around the hoop.
- Let one person march inside the hoop while the others are marching around the hoop. Take turns.
- Jump over the hoop.
- Walk on the rim of the hoop.
- Have the children stand close together in a circle. Let the children take turns rolling the hoop around the circle.
- If you have more than one hoop, play the above games in various combinations, such as "Jump in and out of the first hoop and then walk around the rim of the second one."

RECREATION

BOOKS

DON FREEMAN — *CORDUROY*
SATOMI ICHIKAWA — *LET'S PLAY*
LEO LIONNI — *ALEXANDER AND THE WIND-UP MOUSE*

CAMPING

FOR OPENERS

CAMPING IS A RECREATION ENJOYED BY MANY FAMILIES. TALK WITH THE CHILDREN ABOUT THEIR EXPERIENCES AND THEN PLAN A PRETEND TRIP WITH THEM.

"TODAY WE ARE GOING TO PACK FOR A CAMPING TRIP. IF I CAN'T REMEMBER SOME OF THE CAMPING WORDS, MAYBE YOU CAN HELP ME. FIRST WE NEED TO GET THOSE BAGS THAT YOU USE TO SLEEP IN. THEY'RE CALLED_____. THAT'S RIGHT, THEY'RE CALLED SLEEPING BAGS. WE ALSO WILL NEED SOMETHING TO STAY IN AT NIGHT OR IF IT RAINS. IT'S MADE OF CLOTH. I THINK THEY ARE CALLED CAMP HOUSES. NO, _____. THAT'S RIGHT, TENTS. WHAT CAN WE TAKE TO COOK OUR MEALS ON? _____. A CAMPING STOVE, YOU'RE RIGHT. WHAT DO YOU LIGHT THOSE WITH? _____. THANK YOU. LET'S SEE, WHAT ELSE WILL WE NEED? (USE THE IDEAS THE CHILDREN THINK OF TO CONTINUE THE STORY. REMEMBER THEY MIGHT TAKE DIFFERENT ITEMS THAN YOU WOULD. AFTER THE CHILDREN HAVE ALL EXPRESSED THEMSELVES PACK THE CAR.) SOUNDS LIKE WE HAVE EVERYTHING WE NEED FOR A GREAT CAMPING TRIP. LET'S LOAD THE CAR. (GO AROUND THE CIRCLE AND LET EACH CHILD REMEMBER ONE OF THE CAMPING ITEMS. THE CHILD CAN TAKE THAT ITEM TO THE CAR.) ROMMEL, YOU TAKE THE _____. GREG, YOU GET THE _____. THE CAR'S ALL LOADED. OFF WE GO!"

FINGERPLAYS

FOREST FUN

Worms and germs and rainy days,
Or even tents that drip,
Skunks and stumps and mosquito stings
Won't ruin our camping trip.

We're hardy forest campers
Prepared for nature's wrath,
But after a three day week-end,
We're ready for a bath.
                    Dick Wilmes

ANIMALS

Can you hop like a rabbit?
Can you jump like a frog?
Can you walk like a duck?
Can you run like a dog?
Can you swim like a fish?
Can you sit by a campfire?
Just like this?
(Ask the children if they have seen these animals on their camping trips.)

FINGERPLAYS

BY THE CAMPFIRE

We sat around the campfire
On a chilly night,
Telling spooky stories
In the pale moonlight.

Then we added some more logs
To make the fire bright,
And sang some favorite camp songs
Together with all our might.

And when the fire flickered
And embers began to form,
We snuggled in our sleeping bags
All cozy, tired, and warm.
Dick Wilmes

A LITTLE GIRL'S (BOY'S) WALK

A little girl went walking,
One lovely summer day.
She saw a little rabbit,
That quickly ran away.

She saw a shining river,
Go winding in and out,
And little fishes in it,
Were swimming all about.

RECIPES

APPLE RINGS

YOU'LL NEED

10 apples
Pam
Plastic Wrap

TO MAKE: Peel apples and remove the cores. Slice into rings. Place on a lightly greased cookie sheet or on clear, plastic wrap which has been laid on a cookie sheet. Dry in an electric oven at low or warm temperature; in a gas oven use only the pilot light for heat. Drying takes 6-9 hours, making this a good overnight project. The apples need not be dried to a crisp.

From A FAMILY AFFAIR: SNACKS by Aviva Croll

CAMPING CANDLES

YOU'LL NEED

Apples
Bananas
Cherries
Lettuce

TO MAKE: Core the apples and then cut in half crossways to form candle stands. Peel the bananas and cut them in half to form short 'candles'. Place the bananas in the apple bases and put on a bed of lettuce. Top the candle off by adding a big red cherry to the top. While you're enjoying your salad, talk about what you'd do if suddenly the lights went out.

RECREATION

CLASSROOM VISITOR

● Have a senior boy/girl scout or a leader come and tell the children about camping trips that the scout group has taken. If the person has pictures or movies of the trips, take time for everyone to enjoy them. After the movies or pictures are shown, talk about the different pieces of equipment, what types of recreation the scouts were doing, how they cooked their food, and where they slept.

LANGUAGE GAMES

TALK ABOUT

Have the children sit around a big picnic blanket. Talk about the times when they have gone on a camping trip or have been on a picnic in the forest preserve. When talking about camping, ask questions like:
"Where did you sleep?"
"Where did you eat?"
"What did you eat?"
"How did you fix your food?"
"Where was the bathroom?"
"Did you see any animals? What kind?"

CAMPING
EQUIPMENT

Have different pieces of camping equipment available to show the children — canteen, portable stove, sleeping bag, tent, backpack, and so on. Discuss the name and function of each piece. Maybe some of the children have used camping equipment. Let them tell about it.
EXTENSION:
● Put camping catalogues in the language area and convert the dramatic play area into a campground by using the camping equipment that you have gathered.
● Get a large white sheet and divide it into as many sections as you have pieces of camping equipment. Put one piece of equipment into each section. Sitting around the sheet, have a child toss a beanbag into one of the sections and then name and tell about the piece of camping equipment in that section.

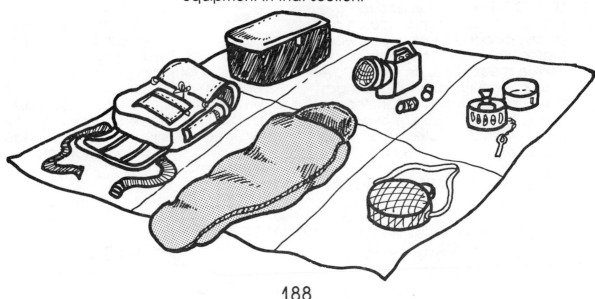

ACTIVE GAMES

PARACHUTE PLAY

Going on a 'nature hike' is one of the most popular things to do on a camping trip.

Have the children stand around the parachute. *"We're going on a 'nature hike'. Remember we must walk slowly and quietly so that we do not disturb the animals.* (Walk on tiptoes slowly around the circle looking at the nature.) *Oh! Look, there is a bear. It is lumbering across the forest path.* (Lumber like the bear and then tiptoe again.) *I'm glad that it did not see us. It was so big. What color was the bear's fur? Let's keep looking for other things as we walk.* (Walk and look.) *Look up, there is a flock of geese flying overhead.* (Pick up the parachute and wave it like the wings of geese and then begin walking again.) *I'm glad that it is a nice, warm day. There is just a little breeze blowing so that we do not get too hot.* (Wave the parachute like a quiet breeze and then walk.) *I'm sure that the animals like the breeze too. Let's see if we can see anything crawling or hopping on the ground.* (Let the children name bugs, animals, etc. that they see. Make the parachute move like that bug or animal. After they have had the opportunity to make the parachute move like a variety of animals, put the parachute down, and go back to the campsite.) *It's getting dark, we need to get back to the campground."*

SINGING

Make a pretend 'campfire' by putting large blocks in the middle of the circle time area. Choose several favorite songs to sing and then let the children choose some that they would like to sing.

BOOKS

JAN WAHL — *DOCTOR RABBIT'S LOST SCOUT*
VERA WILLIAMS — *THREE DAYS ON A RIVER IN A RED CANOE*
JANE YOLEN — *GIANTS GO CAMPING*

RECREATION

TRANSPORTATION

FOR OPENERS

HAVE MODELS OF ALL TYPES OF TRANSPORTATION. NAME EACH FORM AND TALK ABOUT THE COLOR, SHAPE, AND SIZE OF EACH VEHICLE. THEN GIVE A MODEL TO EACH CHILD. SAY, "THOSE OF YOU WHO HAVE A CAR, COUNT HOW MANY WHEELS ARE ON IT." HAVE A CHILD TELL THE GROUP HOW MANY WHEELS S/HE COUNTED. "THOSE WHO HAVE BOATS STAND UP. TELL US WHAT COLORS ARE ON YOUR BOAT." LET EACH CHILD NAME THE COLORS ON HIS / HER BOAT. CONTINUE BY ASKING DIFFERENT QUESTIONS ABOUT THE VEHICLES.

FINGERPLAYS

THE BOAT
Some boats are big.
Some boats are small.
Some boats have motors.
Some have none at all.
Some boats you can live in.
Some boats are for play.
Whatever your boat,
Be safe all the day.

THE AIRPLANE
The airplane has great big wings,
It's motor spins around and sings,
"VVVVVVVVVVVVVVVVVVVVV!!!"

The airplane goes up.
The airplane goes high.
The airplane flies down,
From way up in the sky.

OUR FAMILY CAR
This is our family car,
The engine purrs like new.
Four wheels and a body,
It is painted blue.

Dad uses it for business,
Or to drive us to the store.
We take it on vacation.
You couldn't ask for more.

In the winter weather,
If we should miss the bus,
We can still get to our school,
In the family car we trust.
Dick Wilmes

THE TRAIN
I go on a train
That runs on the track.
It takes me to Grandmother's
And then comes back.

190

RECIPES

Pretend you're eating a snack on an airplane or having a snack in the car.

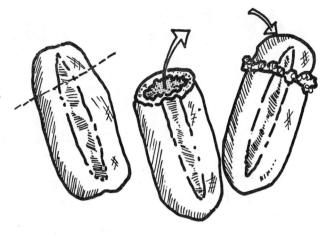

STUFFED BUNS

Pretend you've stopped for lunch on your vacation.

YOU'LL NEED

Your favorite sandwich fillings
A Kaiser roll for each sandwich

TO MAKE: Make your favorite sandwich fillings such as tuna fish salad or egg salad. Cut the top ¼ off each bun. Scoop the bread out of the bottom ¾ of each bun. Put the filling into the hollowed out part of the bread. Put the top ¼ back on and eat.

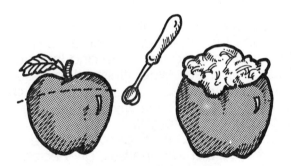

STUFFED APPLES

YOU'LL NEED

½ cup peanut butter
¼ cup rice cereal
1 carrot, grated
5 apples

TO MAKE: Mix the peanut butter, rice cereal, and grated carrot. Slice a ½ inch piece from the top of the apple. With a melon baller, scoop out the core and fill the cavity with the peanut butter mixture.

From A FAMILY AFFAIR: SNACKS by Aviva Croll

FIELD TRIPS

• Tour the bus or train depot nearest your center.

• Take a ride. Have each child bring a picnic lunch or snack with him/her. Get on the bus (train). Get off at a stop near a park. Walk over to the park, play for awhile and then eat. Walk back to the bus (train) stop and return home.

LANGUAGE GAMES

VEHICLE
SOUNDS

Talk about the different sounds that transportation vehicles make. After the children are familiar with a variety of vehicle sounds, get the tape recorder out and let them make their favorite sound into the recorder. Play the tape back and let the children guess what sound is playing and who is making it.

RECREATION

LANGUAGE GAMES

TAKING A TRIP
Let the children pretend that they are going on a trip. Say, *"If I were going on a trip, I'd visit _____."* Then let each of the children have the opportunity to tell where s/he would go or who s/he might visit. Encourage further discussion by asking what s/he would do at that place or say to the person s/he is visiting.

SAFETY
Have a large picture of a car. Talk about all of the *'safety rules'* when riding in a automobile. Then talk about *'safety rules'* when riding in other forms of transportation such as a train, airplane, motor boat, etc. Let the children enjoy creating ways to be *'safe'* on a rocket ship.

POSITION WORDS
Have a large model of a bus and enough miniature people for each child. Give each child at least one person. Go around the circle giving directions to each child about where to put his/her person in relation to the bus. For example, *"Jamie, put your person under the bus."* or *"Matthew, put your person in front of the bus."*
EXTENSION:
- When finished, pass the people out again. Ask the children to think of a place that their person could be going on the bus. Quickly walk around the circle and let each child whisper the place in your ear. When finished say, *"So many exciting places to go! I could go _____. (Name as many as you can remember.)Did I forget any?"* Have the children name the places that you forgot.
- Make a large felt car and a small felt gingerbread type person for each child. As you did with the bus, give each child directions as to where to put his/her person in relationship to the car. For example, *"Ian, put your person in the car."*

ACTIVE GAMES

CREATIVE
MOVEMENT

As you discuss various modes of transportation, let the children pretend to be a vehicle or driving a certain type of vehicle.

AIRPLANE: Have the children stand up and fly like an airplane. Airplanes take-off, fly slowly and quickly, turn, dive, and come in for landings.

TRAIN: Have everybody line up behind one another. Put both hands on the person's waist in front of you to form a train. Take a *'pretend'* trip to a favorite spot. It's a long trip. The tracks go outside, down the halls, and through the other rooms in the building. Make stops along the way to pick-up passengers, drop them off, and see the scenes.

CAR: Pretend that you are driving the car to the park. The family is going to spend the afternoon there. You have already eaten lunch, but you did bring a snack for later. As you are driving, talk about what you will do at the park.

SPACESHIP: The spaceship part of the rocket is pointed. Have the children put their hands in a *'V-shape'* over their head. When they *'blast-off'* it is very powerful. As they reach *'orbit'* they glide smoothly through the atmosphere to their destination. *"How does it feel to land? What position will you be in when you land?"* Once they have answered these questions, have them *'land'*. Reverse the trip and come back to *'Earth'*.

BOAT: Make *'captain's hats'* at art. Have the children bring them to circle time. Put on your *'captain's hat'* This will show the *'passengers'* that you are in charge of the sightseeing boat and know how to drive it safely. Today you are going on an excursion across a lake to a beautiful island. As you are maneuvering the boat, talk about the homes on the shore, the wildlife that you see, other boats on the lake, and scenes along the way.

ACTIVE GAMES

SINGING

THE WHEELS ON THE BUS

The wheels on the bus go 'round and 'round,
'Round and 'round, 'round and 'round.
The wheels on the bus go 'round and 'round,
All through the town.

(Suit the actions
to the words.)

The people on the bus go up and down,
Up and down, up and down.
The people on the bus go up and down,
All through the town.

The money on the bus goes clink, clink, clink,
Clink, clink, clink.
The money on the bus goes clink, clink, clink,
All through the town

The driver on the bus says, "Move on back," etc.

The children on the bus say, "Yak, yak, yak," etc.

The mothers on the bus say, "Sh, sh, sh," etc.

The wipers on the bus go swish, swish, swish, etc.

The horn on the bus goes honk, honk, honk, etc.

The wheels on the bus go 'round and 'round,
'Round and 'round, 'round and 'round.
The wheels on the bus go 'round and 'round,
All through the town.

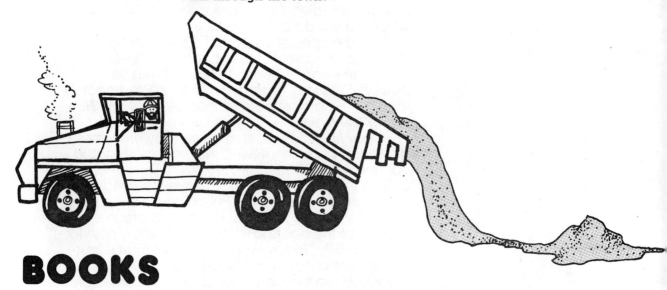

BOOKS

SYLVIA TESTER — *TRAFFIC JAM*
GEORGE ZAFFO —*AIRPLANES & TRUCKS & TRAINS, FIRE ENGINES & BOATS & SHIPS,
& BUILDINGS & WRECKING MACHINES*

CARNIVAL

FOR OPENERS

A CARNIVAL IS "*AN ATTRACTION OFFERING RIDES, SHOWS, CATERING, AND GAMING CONCESSIONS. UNLIKE THE CIRCUS, AUDIENCE ENTERTAINMENT IS BY 'PARTICIPATION' INSTEAD OF 'WITNESSING'.*"*

BEFORE CIRCLE TIME, GET A PAPER BAG AND FILL IT WITH THINGS THAT YOU MIGHT SEE AT THE CARNIVAL: TOY CARS, MILK BOTTLES, TARGETS AND BALLS, STUFFED DOLLS, PICTURES (OR PLASTIC MODELS) OF DIFFERENT FOODS, HORSES, BINGO CARDS, AND SO ON.

TALK WITH THE CHILDREN FOR SEVERAL MINUTES ABOUT CARNIVALS. SEE HOW MANY OF THEM HAVE EVER BEEN TO A CARNIVAL. THEN SAY, "IN THIS BAG I HAVE STATUES, DOLLS, PICTURES, AND OTHER THINGS THAT YOU MIGHT SEE AT A CARNIVAL. I'M GOING TO TAKE THEM OUT ONE AT A TIME. AS I DO, YOU CAN TELL US IF YOU HAVE EVER SEEN THESE THINGS AT A CARNIVAL." TAKE THE ITEMS OUT, DISCUSSING THE CHILDREN'S EXPERIENCES AS YOU DO.

EXTENSION: AFTER CIRCLE TIME, PUT THESE ITEMS ON THE DISCOVERY TABLE FOR THE CHILDREN TO EXPLORE.

*FROM CIRCUS WORLD, BARABOO, WISCONSIN

FINGERPLAYS

RIDING THE MERRY-GO-ROUND
Ride with me on the merry-go-round,
Around and around and around.
Up the horses go, up
Down the horses go, down!
You ride a horse that is white.
I'll ride a horse that is brown.
Up and down on the merry-go-round.
Our horses go around and around.

RECREATION

FINGERPLAYS

AT THE CARNIVAL

The barkers are busy,
Calling their game,
"Three tosses a quarter—
You lose! What a shame!"

The lights are all flashing.
It's almost a dream.
You had pop and peanuts,
And now it's ice cream.

The Merry-Go-Round is moving.
The music is loud.
It's always exciting.
There's always a crowd.

It's fun at the carnival.
It happens each year.
When summer comes around
And vacation is here.
                    Dick Wilmes

THE FERRIS WHEEL

The ferris wheel goes up so high,
You think you're going to touch the sky.
And down you come and then around,
Spinning up above the ground.
And when it's over, you are so proud,
To think you almost touched a cloud.
                    Dick Wilmes

RECIPES

TACOS

YOU'LL NEED

24 corn tortillas
3 pounds of extra lean ground beef
6 tomatoes
½ head of lettuce
1 bunch of Cilantro or Coriander
1 pound Jack or Cheddar Cheese
2 medium onions

TO MAKE: Cook the meat and drain the excess fat. Chop together 1 onion and 2 tomatoes. Add these vegetables to the meat and simmer. Chop the other 4 tomatoes, 1 onion, and the cilantro or coriander together to make the sauce. Shred the lettuce and grate the cheese. Place the ingredients in this order on a folded tortilla: meat, lettuce, sauce, and sprinkle with cheese. This makes about 24 tacos.
from A FAMILY AFFAIR: SNACKS
by Aviva Croll

OLD FASHIONED LEMONADE

YOU'LL NEED

2 lemons
3 to 4 T. light honey
3½ to 4 cups water
lots of ice cubes

TO MAKE: Cut the lemons in half. Squeeze the juice from each lemon on a lemon juicer. Dissolve the honey in the lemon juice. Add the water to the lemon mixture. Pour into a glass with lots of ice. Serves 6.
from COME AND GET IT
by Kathleen Baxter

LANGUAGE GAMES

SPINNER FUN   Make 'carnival-type' spinner games. Get large pieces of posterboard and draw a big circle on each one. Attach an arrow to the middle of each circle with a large brad. The arrow should be firm, but loose enough to spin easily. Divide the circle into as many sections as you need. For example you need 26 sections if you play 'Know Your Alphabet', 10 sections if you play 'Counting', or 8 sections if you play 'Basic Colors'. Make as many games as your children would enjoy. During circle time let the children take turns spinning the arrow while the remaining children call out where the arrow is pointing.

FAVORITE RIDES   Have pictures of carnivals. Discuss the games, rides, foods, and so on. Ask the children what rides they have been on, who went with them, how they felt, and would they like to go again?
EXTENSION:
Ask the children what their favorite ride was. See if they all liked the same ride or a variety of different ones. After you have discussed each ride, let the children pretend to be on that ride. They can do it at their place in the circle or move around as they go.

PAINT A BACKDROP   Tack a long sheet of newsprint or butcher paper onto the playground fence. Put a variety of tempera colors into juice cans and carry them outside in an 'eight-pack' soda container. Put the paint and brushes near the paper. Throughout the day, let the children enjoy painting a colorful 'backdrop' for the carnival. When dry, hang the mural near the circle time area, in the dramatic play or language center.

ACTIVE GAMES

MERRY-GO
ROUND ANIMALS

At art, have the children make the 'head' for their 'merry-go-round animal' by decorating a large paper bag. Collect enough brooms so that each child can have one. Put the decorated bags over the brooms to make 'merry-go-round animals.' Using chalk, mark off a large circle in the circle time area or outside if the weather permits. Let the children enjoy riding around and around, up and down while the music is playing.

CARS

Another popular ride at the carnival is 'cars' or 'fire engines' that go around the track. Let the children pretend that they are vehicles by squatting down and moving around the circle. They can make the noise of their vehicle and steer with their hands. Have one child act as the operator who turns the ride on and off.

LET'S GO
FISHING

Make a 'fishing pole' for each child by tying one end of a string to a dowel rod and the other end to a small magnet. On different days of the unit, have the 'lake' full of different categories of 'fish'. (The 'lake' is the middle of the circle time area.) For example, make a 'school of fish' with different shapes drawn on them, 'fish' showing different feelings, or 'fish' with pictures of people doing activities.

At the beginning of the game, have all of the children 'fish'. When they have caught a 'fish' have them sit back down. Play games with the 'fish' that the children have caught. For example, have a child hold up a 'fish' with a shape on it and the remainder of the children call out what shape it is or have each child tell what feeling is drawn on his/her 'fish'.

BOOKS

NATALIE CARLSON —*MARIE-LOUISE & CHRISTOPE AT THE CARNIVAL*
DONALD CREWS —*CAROUSEL*

CIRCUS

FOR OPENERS

OF ALL OF THE MAGNIFICENT CIRCUS ACTS, CHILDREN OF ALL AGES SEEM TO ENJOY THE CLOWNS MOST OF ALL. JUST WHEN YOU THINK YOU HAVE SEEN EVERY TRICK, ALONG COMES A CLOWN OR TWO TO MAKE YOU LAUGH AGAIN. TEACH THE CHILDREN THIS SONG AT THE BEGINNING AND ENJOY IT OFTEN WHILE TALKING ABOUT CIRCUSES. SING TO THE TUNE OF *"I'M A LITTLE TEAPOT"*.

> I'M A LITTLE CLOWN WHO'S SHORT AND FAT,
> HERE IS MY TUMMY, HERE IS MY HAT.
> I CAN DO A TRICK AS YOU WILL SEE,
> JUST TURN AROUND AND LOOK AT ME.

AFTER YOU SING THE LAST LINE, HAVE EVERYONE TURN AROUND. POINT TO ONE OF THE CHILDREN. THAT CHILD CAN DO A TRICK. SING THE SONG AGAIN AND LET ANOTHER CHILD DO A TRICK.

FINGERPLAYS

ELEPHANT
Right foot, left foot, see me go.
I am gray and big and slow.
Here I come walking down the street,
With my trunk and four big feet.

CLOWNS
This little clown is fat and gay.
This little clown does tricks all day.
This little clown is tall and strong.
This little clown sings a funny song.
This little clown is wee and small.
But he can do anything at all.

THE CIRCUS
With clowns that play
And elephants that sway,
The circus came to town today.
　　　　　　　Dick Wilmes

THE CIRCUS COMES TO TOWN
The circus comes to town today,
With wagons big and bright.
The posters and the banners say,
"A SPECIAL PERFORMANCE TONIGHT"

The circus parade is about to begin.
It goes right through the town,
With cages of tigers, lions, and bears,
It will be led by the clown.

I'll go to see the circus tonight,
To watch as the trapeze swings,
To see the wire walker,
And jugglers do their things.

Twas hard to wait all day long
When in a field so near,
Were camels and monkeys, elephants, too.
It's the best day of the year!!
　　　　　　　Dick Wilmes

RECIPES

FROZEN BANANA ON A STICK

YOU'LL NEED

Bananas
Popsicle sticks
Crushed pecans or grape nuts
Cinnamon
Nutmeg

TO MAKE: Peel the banana and insert the popsicle stick. Dip the banana in milk and roll in the nutty mixture. Wrap in plastic and freeze.

from A FAMILY AFFAIR: SNACKS by Aviva Croll

CRACKER JACKS

YOU'LL NEED

3 to 4 quarts of popcorn
½ cup of butter
½ to 1 t. of molasses
⅓ cup of honey
1 cup of peanuts

TO MAKE: Melt the butter over a low heat, add molasses and honey. (This will turn into caramel after it bakes.) Divide the mixture in half and mix with 2 quarts of popcorn. Put in a large cake pan. Mix the other half and spread it in another cake pan. Bake the cracker jacks at 350 degrees for 10 to 12 minutes. Stir once while baking. Let cool for crispness.

from COME AND GET IT by Kathleen Baxter

ICE CREAM CONE CAKE

YOU'LL NEED

12 flat bottomed cones
2 eggs
4 T. honey
1 cup whole wheat flour
2 cups yellow corn meal
1 t. salt
1 rounded t. baking soda
2 cups buttermilk
2 T. vegetable oil

TO MAKE: Beat the eggs and honey together. Measure and sift the dry ingredients. Mix alternately with the milk. After everything is well mixed, add the oil. Pour the batter into the ice cream cones. (Fill about ¾ full.) Put the cones on a cookie sheet. Bake them at 425 degrees for about 30 minutes. Frost with a little honey and serve.

from COME AND GET IT by Kathleen Baxter

FIELD TRIPS

- Make arrangements for your class to visit the local YMCA/YWCA or other gym facility and watch one of the tumbling or acrobatic classes for young children. If possible, make additional arrangements for your class to participate and do some tumbling.

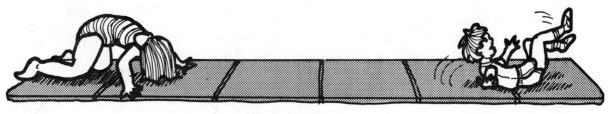

LANGUAGE GAMES

TALK ABOUT
Say the word 'circus'. Have the children tell you all of the words that come to their minds when they think about circuses. As the children say the words, write them on a large sheet of paper. Encourage them to think of as many words as possible. When they have finished, go back to each word and talk about it. After circle time, hang the list up for the parents to enjoy.

COLORFUL CLOWNS
Get a large picture of a clown's face. Talk about the make-up, the clown's job, why s/he is funny, and so on. Give the children the opportunity to tell about clowns that they have seen. After the discussion, have the children look carefully at the clown's face. Name all the colors that the clown used to make-up his/her face.
EXTENSION:
Have a volunteer come to class and put make-up on the children. (Remember that some of the children will not want to be made-up.)

CIRCUS ANIMALS
Buy several boxes of animal cookies. Pass one box around and have the children each take a cookie. When each child has one, let him/her name the animal s/he is holding. After each animal has been identified, categorize them in a variety of different ways. Say:
"All of you who have circus animals, stand up."
Have the children name their animal and then sit down.
"All of you who have animals that roar, stand up."
Have the children name the animal and then sit back down.
"Those who have animals with four legs, stand up and clap four times."
Continue as above.

CIRCUS PERFORMERS
Collect a variety of circus props and accessories such as stools, buckets, rope, long stick (broom handle), whip, costumes, balls, and others you may have. Put them in the middle of the circle. Have a child go and pick out one of the props. Have the children think of all of the people in the circus who might use that prop and how they would use it. Remember that many of the props will be used by a variety of performers.

201

ACTIVE GAMES

MOVING   Have the children move around the room like different *'circus animals'*:

      LIONS — *Stalk*
      ELEPHANTS — *Lumber*
      HORSES — *Gallop*
      DOGS — *Run*
      MONKEYS — *Jump and roll around on the ground*
      GORILLAS — *Stretch and pound their chests*

EXTENSION:

After the children know how circus animals move, they can begin to do tricks. Have hula hoops available. Jump through them like the fierce *'lions'*, roll them like the *'elephants'*, sit in them like the *'dogs'*, and so on. Have brooms. The *'horses'* and *'zebras'* jump over them, the *'elephants'* walk over them, *'dogs'* pick them up and run away with them.

BALLOON BOUNCE   Blow up several large circus balloons. Play some circus music while the children try to keep the balloons up in the air. If a balloon falls to the ground, pick it up and begin again. Let the balloons float to the ground when the music stops.

FOLLOW THE RING MASTER   Pretend to be the *'Ring Master'*. Say *"LADIES AND GENTLEMEN, CHILDREN OF ALL AGES, today we are going to do circus tricks. Listen carefully as I give you the directions."* Have the children do a variety of tricks, such as:

- Roll like the clowns.
- Balance on the high-wire like the tight-rope walkers.
- Jump like the trampoline artists.
- March like the members of the band.
- Swing like the trapeze artist.
- Fence with the lions and tigers like the wild animal tamer.

BOOKS

DICK BRUNA — *CIRCUS*
BETSY MAESTRO — *A BUSY DAY*
BETSY MAESTRO — *HARRIET GOES TO THE CIRCUS*
BRIAN WILDSMITH — *CIRCUS*

PARADES

FOR OPENERS

ENJOY READING THIS POEM TO THE CHILDREN. GET THEM INVOLVED WITH EACH STANZA BY MAKING THE NOISE OR THE MOTION OF THE ACTIVITY BEING HIGHLIGHTED.

TOWN PARADE

The people are beside the street,
All standing in the sun.
I hear the noon whistle blowing,   (Have the children blow the whistle.)
The parade has just begin.

First I hear police cars,
Sirens going "Vrrrum, Vrrrum!"   (Be police cars in the parade.)
Driving slowly up the street,
Trying to make some room.

Next there comes the ambulance
Yellow as it can be.
With the paramedics ready,   (Drive the ambulance, looking alert.)
In case of emergency.

Followed by the fire trucks,
The horns and whistles scream.   (Be fire trucks blowing their horns.)
And hanging all along the rail,
Is the proud firefighting team.

Now there comes the color guard,
Scouts are marching proud.
Carrying the flags we all know,   (Pretend to hold a large flag. It is heavy.)
Presenting them to the crowd

The motorcycle troop is next,
You can hear them roar and zoom.   (Drive trick motorcycles.
As they weave and turn about,   remember their noise.)
There hardly's any room.

Soon we see a tiny car,
Putting up the street.   (Pretend the circle time area is the
Out jumps fourteen clowns,   small car. Everyone squish together
Each with great big feet.   like the clowns.)

Don't forget the bands and such,
Making music fine.   (Play your favorite instrument.)
Drums and horns and cymbols play,
All marching in a line.

There are floats that carry people,
A car to drive the queen.   (Sitting cross-legged, go around and
People riding horseback,   around like the brushes on
And a street sweeping machine.   the street sweeper.)

Finally comes the last police car,
The music starts to fade.
We had a nice afternoon,
Watching the town parade.   (Wave good-bye to the parade.)
                    Dick Wilmes

RECREATION

203

FINGERPLAYS

THE BAND

Listen to the band parade,
Little snare drums swell and fade.
Rat-a-tat-tat, rat-a-tat-tat,
Rat-a-tat, tat, tat.

Down the street the marchers come,
I can hear the big old drum.
Br-r-r-rum, br-r-r-rum,
Br-r-r-rum, br-r-r-rum.

Flutes are playing shrill and high,
As the players go parading by.
Deedle-dee, deedle-dee,
Deedle-dee, deedle-dee.

The big bassoons rumble and roar,
Deep bass notes out of them pour.
Rumble-rum, rumble-rum,
Rumble-rum-rum.

I can hear the trumpets, too,
Sounding clear and loud and true.
Toot-a-toot-too, toot-a-toot-too,
Toot-a-toot-too-too-too.

Slide trombones sound loud and sweet,
As the band marches down the street.
Tra-dum, tra-dum, tra-tra-tra.
Tra-dum, tra-dum, dum, dum.

DRUMS

Boom, boom, boom,
Goes the big brass drum.
Rat-a-tat goes the little one.
And down the street in line we come,
To the boom, boom, boom,
Of the big brass drum,
And the rat-a-tat of the little one.

RECIPES

POCKET SANDWICHES

YOU'LL NEED

Pita bread
Shredded lettuce
Chopped tomato
Small pieces of chicken or turkey
Salad dressing

TO MAKE: Combine the lettuce, tomato,
dressing, and meat. Cut the pita bread
in half and fill with the salad mixture.
*from A FAMILY AFFAIR: SNACKS
by Aviva Croll*

WATERMELON WEDGES

YOU'LL NEED

Watermelon

TO MAKE: Cut the watermelon into
wedges. Let the children take the
seeds out. Enjoy on a warm day.

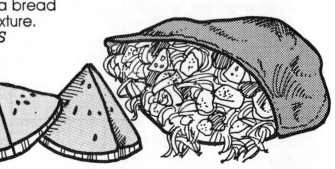

LANGUAGE GAMES

NAME IT — Make a list of all of the things that the children have seen in parades. Have the list for everyone to read and enjoy.

HERE COMES THE PARADE — Have a bag full of statues and models of things and people that would be in a parade, such as *police, police cars, motorcycles, firefighters, fire trucks, clowns, musical instruments, cars, horses, flags, dogs, ambulances, whistles,* and so on.

Pull out the models one at a time. As you pull each model out, have the children name it. Display each one in front of you. After all of the models have been named, make a *'parade line'*. Say, *"Which one of these things would be first in a 'real' parade?"* Continue until the *'parade'* is formed.

EXTENSION:
• Have each child choose one person, animal, or vehicle s/he would like to be in a parade. Have the children line up and have a parade around the school.
• Put all of the statues and models on the manipulative shelf or in the dramatic play center.

RIDDLES — People often take binoculars to parades. Have the children make *'binoculars'* by cupping their hands and then putting them up to their eyes.

Pretend that there is a *'parade'* passing through the classroom. As each entry in the parade comes into focus, say a riddle about it and have the children guess what it is. When they guess, have them look at it closely through their *'binoculars.'*

ACTIVE GAMES

BALLOONS

Colorful balloons are part of every parade. Have a deflated balloon at circle time. Tell the children to watch carefully as you blow it up. Then begin to blow. *"What is happening?"* (Answer.) Continue to blow. *"The balloon is getting bigger and bigger. What would happen to the balloon if you stuck it with a pin?"* (Answer.) *"What would happen if you just let it go?"* Have the children watch carefully as you let the balloon go. Talk again. *"Did the balloon do what you thought it would?"* Blow the balloon up again and tie it. Let it float around.

   Now let the children pretend to be colorful balloons. First let each child tell what color s/he is, then get ready to 'blow them up'. As you blow, each child pretends to be a 'balloon' which is getting bigger and bigger. When they are all 'blown up', quickly go and tie each closed and let them 'float' around the room. After they have 'floated', walk to each one and prick him/her. *"POP!!"*

EXTENSION:

* Blow up the 'balloons' again. This time do not tie them shut. Simply have them let out their air and 'fizzle' to the ground.
* At art make all colors of 'balloons' and let the 'balloon man' on the bulletin board hold them all.

BOOKS

ED EMBERELY — *PARADE BOOK*
PETER SPIER — *CRASH! BANG! BOOM!*

MUSICAL INSTRUMENTS

FOR OPENERS

ARRANGE WITH THE LOCAL JUNIOR HIGH OR HIGH SCHOOL BAND DIRECTOR TO HAVE FIVE OR SIX STUDENTS VISIT YOUR CLASS. HAVE THE STUDENTS EACH BRING ONE OR TWO OF THEIR FAVORITE INSTRUMENTS. EACH STUDENT SHOULD BE PREPARED TO TELL SOMETHING ABOUT THE INSTRUMENT S/HE HAS BROUGHT AND THEN PLAY A SHORT, FAMILIAR SONG ON IT FOR THE YOUNG CHILDREN. AFTER EACH STUDENT HAS PLAYED THE SONG, HAVE THE YOUNG CHILDREN GUESS WHAT SONG WAS PLAYED. IF ANY OF THE CHILDREN KNOW THE WORDS, HAVE THE STUDENT PLAY IT AGAIN AND LET THE CHILDREN SING ALONG. A FEW SUGGESTIONS FOR SONGS ARE: ROW, ROW, ROW YOUR BOAT, LONDON BRIDGE'S, FROSTY THE SNOWMAN, HAPPY BIRTHDAY, JINGLE BELLS, AND HOKEY-POKEY.

FINGERPLAYS

MUSIC IN OUR HOME

Mother plays the violin.
Daddy plays the flute.
Big brother blows the horn
Toot-toot-toot-toot-toot.

Little sister keeps the beat
By clanging on a pot.
And I try to sing along
Whether I know the words or not.

THE KITCHEN BAND

Won't you join our band and play?
Wouldn't you like to join today?
With pots and pans we bang away.
I didn't hear you. What did you say?
Dick Wilmes

RECREATION

FINGERPLAYS

THE BODY BAND

Beat, beat with your feet,
We're playing the body band.

Strum, strum with your thumb,
It's the best one in the land.

Clap, clap on your lap,
Keep rhythm with your knees.

Hear, hear with your ear,
Stop laughing if you please.

Cluck, cluck like a duck,
It's fun on a rainy day.

Pop, pop on your top,
Keep humming as you play.

Moan, moan all alone,
You're playing your solo now.

Haste, haste with your waist,
It's time to take your bow!
Dick Wilmes

MY HORN

When I play my little horn,
I put my fingers so —
And then I lift it to my mouth,
And blow, and blow, and blow.

RECIPES

CELERY FLUTES

YOU'LL NEED

Whole strips of celery
Cream cheese or peanut butter
Raisins or peanuts

TO MAKE: Clean the celery. Stuff the celery. Add the peanuts or raisins to make the keys. Before eating let the children pretend to play a song on their flute. Then enjoy eating it.

CLASSROOM VISITOR

● Have parents who play instruments visit your class. Have them bring their instruments with them. If practical, let the children have the opportunity to play the instrument under the guidance of the parent. This is a wonderful opportunity for the children to see first hand how many different ways there are to make music.

LANGUAGE GAMES

MR. ROBERTS'
BAND

"Mr. Roberts loved to play many different instruments. He wanted to teach children how to play them with him. He gathered ten children and began his neighborhood band. Michelle and Charlie learned to play drums. (Give two children drums. Let them play.)*Chad liked the triangle, so Mr. Roberts let him learn to keep rhythm with that instrument.* (Give one child a triangle and let him play it.)*Mr. Roberts really enjoyed playing bells. He taught Becky to play them.* (Give one set of bells to a child and she can demonstrate the sounds to the class.)*Amy and Joseph wanted to play the sticks in the band, so Mr. Roberts gave them each a set.* (Give a set of sticks to two children. They can play them together.)*Mr. Roberts had a xylophone which nobody wanted to play at first. Then Mr. Roberts played a song on it for the children. Several children wanted to play it when they heard the beautiful sounds that it made. Mr. Roberts let Andrew learn to play it first, but promised to teach the others to play it also.* (Let a child play it.)*Mr. Roberts had two tambourines. Stacey and Elizabeth learned songs on them.* (Give the tambourines to two children)*Mr. Roberts last instrument was the castanets. It was his favorite instrument and he gave it to Martin to play."* (Let a child stand up and play the castanets.)

   Once the band is formed, let everyone form a parade line and march around the room playing his/her instrument.

PLAY YOUR
INSTRUMENT

Very slowly say a series of words, some of which are names of musical instruments and some of which are not. For example, *"horn, drum, pencil, tambourine, maraca, bread, violin, piano".* When you name an instrument, the children should pretend that they are playing that instrument. When you say a word that is not an instrument, have the children shake their heads '*No*'.

   At art construct homemade instruments.

ACTIVE GAMES

CHARADES

Whisper the name of an instrument to the child sitting next to you. Have him/her stand and pretend s/he is playing the instrument that you whispered. The other children should try to guess what instrument is being acted out. After it is guessed, the child sits down and whispers the name of another instrument to a child sitting next to her/him. Go around the circle so that everybody has a chance to imitate playing an instrument.

HIDE THE INSTRUMENT

Have four or five familiar instruments at circle time. Give one instrument to a child. The remainder of the group should cover its eyes. The child with the instrument should look around the room and pick a place to hide it. S/he should go over to that place, play the instrument, quickly hide it, and return to the circle. When s/he gets back to the circle, s/he should say, *"Open your eyes and look around, until the _____ you have found."* The children then can open their eyes and try to figure out where they heard the sound coming from. The child who finds the instrument brings it back to the circle and has the next turn to hide a different instrument.

SINGING

Enjoy creating verses for this song to the tune of *"OLD McDONALD HAD A FARM"*.

Mr. Roberts had a band,
E-I-E-I-O
And in his band he had a drum
E-I-E-I-O
With a boom, boom here,
And a boom, boom there,
Here a boom, there a boom,
Everywhere a boom, boom.
Mr. Roberts had a band,
E-I-E-I-O.

And in his band he had a horn,

And in his band he had some cymbols,

And in his band he had a trombone,

Continue adding instruments that the children think of.

BOOKS

RACHEL ISADORA — *BEN'S TRUMPET*
BRUCE MCMILLAN — *ALPHABET SYMPHONY*
MIRIAM STECHER & ALICE KANDELL — *MAX THE MUSIC-MAKER*
ROBERT TALLON — *THE THING IN DOLORES' PIANO*

PARTIES

FOR OPENERS

THERE ARE MANY REASONS TO HAVE PARTIES: HOLIDAYS, SPECIAL OCCASIONS, REMEMBRANCES, AND SO ON. ASK THE CHILDREN ON WHAT OCCASIONS THEY HAVE PARTIES IN THEIR HOMES AND WHAT TYPES OF THINGS THEY DO AT THEIR PARTIES.

CHILDREN IN MEXICO OFTEN MAKE PINATAS FOR THEIR PARTIES. MAKE A SIMPLE PINATA WITH THE CHILDREN:

YOU'LL NEED:	TO MAKE:
NEWSPAPER	HAVE THE CHILDREN TEAR NEWSPAPER INTO STRIPS. WHILE
WHEAT PASTE	THEY ARE TEARING, MIX THE WHEAT PASTE IN A LARGE
BALLOON	BOWL AND BLOW UP THE BALLOON. WHEN THE CHILDREN
PAINTS	HAVE TORN ENOUGH STRIPS, BEGIN TO DIP THE STRIPS,
BRUSHES	ONE AT A TIME, INTO THE WHEAT PASTE. RUB OFF THE
LARGE BOWL	EXCESS PASTE AND PLACE THE INDIVIDUAL STRIPS ON THE
ASSORTED	BALLOON. COVER THE ENTIRE BALLOON, LEAVING A 2"
SMALL TOYS	SPACE AROUND THE KNOT. LET THE STRIPS DRY
AND GOODIES	COMPLETELY, USUALLY OVERNIGHT. DO THIS PROCESS

TWO OR THREE MORE TIMES OVERLAPPING THE BALLOON IN DIFFERENT DIRECTIONS. MAKE CERTAIN TO LET EACH LAYER DRY. WHEN TOTALLY DRY, POP THE BALLOON AND PAINT THE PINATA. WHEN THE PAINT IS DRY, FILL THE PINATA WITH SMALL TOYS AND GOODIES.

ATTACH A STRING TO THE PINATA AND HANG IT FROM THE CEILING. LET THE CHILDREN BREAK IT OPEN WITH A STICK SUCH AS A BROOM HANDLE. (BE CERTAIN TO TAKE ALL NECESSARY SAFETY PRECAUTIONS.) LET THE CHILDREN ENJOY THE TOYS AND GOODIES THAT FALL TO THE FLOOR WHEN THE PINATA IS BROKEN.

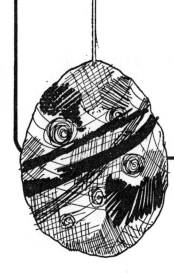

RECREATION

FINGERPLAYS

PARTY TIME

Toot, toot, toot the horns,
Toot them loud and clear,
To tell the children everywhere,
That party time is here.

OUR PARTY

Good morning, Mr. Sunshine,
How are you today?
We're going to have a party
And laugh and sing and play.

RECIPES

MAGIC PIE
YOU'LL NEED

4 eggs
2 cups of milk
½ cup of flour
⅓ cup of butter
1 cup coconut
1 t. vanilla
½ t. nutmeg
a pinch of salt

TO MAKE: Measure everything into a blender, turn on high speed and count to 10. Grease a pie pan, fill with magic mixture. It will settle into layers — crust, custard filling, and coconut topping. Bake at 350 degrees for 40 minutes.
from COME AND GET IT
by Kathleen Baxter

LANGUAGE GAMES

TALK ABOUT

People all over the world enjoy getting together for parties. There are many reasons to have parties. Sometimes these reasons suggest specific decorations, foods, and games and other times they do not.

Talk with the children about different types of parties that they have with their families. Start by discussing birthday parties. Talk about the games that they play, birthday cakes, friends and relatives that they invite, and so on.
EXTENSION:
Go around the circle and have each child clap how old s/he is. As the child is clapping, have the remainder of the children count. When s/he is finished, have another child say how old the child is who did the clapping.

LANGUAGE GAMES

MAKE YOUR TABLECLOTH

Lay a long sheet of butcher paper in the circle time area. Bring markers or crayons.

Have the children sit around the butcher paper. Talk about the different foods that you eat at parties. Then have the children decorate the butcher paper to use as a party tablecloth which can be used at snack and lunch.

PARTY CUBE

Get a square-shaped box. Find six pictures of different types of parties — birthday, Thanksgiving, religious, etc. Glue one picture onto each side of the box. Cover the pictures with clear contact paper.

Roll the cube to a child in the circle. Have him/her tell what type of party the people in the picture are celebrating. Has the child ever been to that type of party? What did s/he do at the party? Has anyone else ever been to a similar party? Have the child roll the cube to another child and continue discussing parties.

PARTY INVITATIONS

Many times people send invitations when they are going to have a party. Before circle time, draw very simple pictures of something that would suggest a certain type of party, such as a heart for a Valentine party, a dreidel for a Hanukkah party, a flag for a Fourth of July picnic, and so on. Put the pictures in envelopes. Write a child's name on each envelope in large print.

At circle time say, *"The letter carrier asked me to deliver these invitations. If the invitation that I hold up belongs to you, come up and get it."* When everyone has an invitation, open them. Let each child have an opportunity to tell what type of party s/he has been invited to.

ACTIVE GAMES

PARACHUTE PLAY

Bring the parachute (sheet) and a tennis ball to circle time. Have a child say how old s/he is and then bounce the ball on the parachute that many times, counting together as you bounce it. Continue until each child has had the opportunity to say his/her age.

BOOKS

PAT HUTCHINS — *SURPRISE PARTY*
EZRA JACK KEATS — *LETTER TO AMY*

RECREATION

FOR SEASONS AND HOLIDAYS

The Circle Time Book

by Liz and Dick Wilmes

The Circle Time Book captures the spirit of seasons and holidays. The big book is filled with more than 400 circle time activities for the preschool classroom. Thirty-nine seasons and holidays are included.

Each season and holiday is introduced with an opening group activity for all children. Following each opening activity, **The Circle Time Book** includes a wide variety of language and active games, songs, fingerplays, creative movement exercises, and lists of related books.

For example, holidays included for September are: First Day of School, Labor Day, Grandparent's Day, Mexican Independence Day, Johnny Appleseed Day, and First Day of Fall.

A useful companion to **Everyday Circle Times.**

ISBN 0-943452-00-7, Building Blocks, 128 pages $8.95

FOR EVERYDAY

Everyday Circle Times

by Liz and Dick Wilmes

Over 900 ideas for Circle Time. This is one of the most important and challenging periods in the children's day. Choose activities from 48 different units. Each unit is introduced with an opening activity, and expanded through language and active games, fingerplays, stories, recipes, books and more.

Just a few of the sections are: Community Helpers, Self-Concept, Animals, Camping, Weather, Colors, Popcorn, Dinosaurs, Transportation, Shapes, Parades, and Machines.

Everyday Circle Times and its companion **The Circle Time Book** are *musts* for every teacher's book shelf.

ISBN 0-943452-01-5, Building Blocks, 216 pages $12.95

AVAILABLE FROM BOOKSTORES, SCHOOL SUPPLY STORES
OR ORDER DIRECTLY FROM:

P.O. BOX 31, DEPT. BK
DUNDEE, IL 60118

Felt Board Fun

by Liz and Dick Wilmes

Make your felt board come alive. Discover how versatile it is as the children become involved with the wide range of activities designed to help them think creatively and learn basic concepts.

This unique book contains over 150 ideas with accompanying patterns. Included are activities for colors, animals, feelings, body awareness, the five senses, letters, numbers, shapes, foods, seasons, and holidays. There is a special section of activities developed specifically for creative thinking skills. **Felt Board Fun** contains a complete index of patterns for your convenience.

This book is truly a great addition to every teacher's resource library.

ISBN 0-943452-02-3, Building Blocks, 224 pages $12.95

FOR YOUR ORDER

NAME _____

ADDRESS _____

CITY _____

STATE _____ ZIP _____

QTY		EACH	TOTAL
____	EVERYDAY CIRCLE TIMES	$12.95	_____
____	THE CIRCLE TIME BOOK	$ 8.95	_____
____	FELT BOARD FUN	$12.95	_____
		TOTAL ORDER	_____